Sparrow iOS Game Framework Beginner's Guide

Create mobile games for iOS devices with the Sparrow iOS game framework

Johannes Stein

BIRMINGHAM - MUMBAI

Sparrow iOS Game Framework Beginner's Guide

First published: June 2014

Production reference: 1180614

Published by Packt Publishing Ltd.
Livery Place
35 Livery Street
Birmingham B3 2PB, UK.

ISBN 978-1-78216-150-9

www.packtpub.com

Cover image by Sujay Gawand (sujaygawand@gmail.com)

Credits

Author

Johannes Stein

Reviewers

James Borden

Alex Harrison

Karuna Krishnasamy

Daniel Sperl

Sladjan Trajkovic

Commissioning Editor

Usha Iyer

Acquisition Editor

Nikhil Karkal

Content Development Editor

Sharvari Tawde

Technical Editors

Pratik More

Ritika Singh

Copy Editors

Sayanee Mukherjee

Deepa Nambiar

Project Coordinator

Binny K. Babu

Proofreaders

Simran Bhogal

Maria Gould

Paul Hindle

Indexers

Rekha Nair

Priya Subramani

Graphics

Abhinash Sahu

Production Coordinator

Nilesh Bambardekar

Cover Work

Nilesh Bambardekar

About the Author

Johannes Stein has been interested in software and game development for most part of his life. He has used a variety of technologies, programming languages, and platforms. In the last few years, he has worked as a freelancer using web and mobile technologies for a number of different companies and start-ups, working on several iOS apps and games. Among the technologies he used were Sparrow, cocos2D, and UIKit. He has co-authored the book *Irrlicht 1.7 Realtime 3D Engine Beginner's Guide* that was published in 2011 by Packt Publishing. He can be followed on Twitter: @Stoney_FD.

I would like to thank everyone who helped me in making this book a reality, specifically everyone involved at Packt for being patient with me and giving me constant and helpful feedback. My thanks go out to all the technical reviewers as well who gave me great pointers and improved the book on multiple levels. Last but not least, I would like to thank my family and friends who tried to motivate me, offering help whenever possible and getting me through a few small rough patches.

About the Reviewers

James Borden is an expat mobile application developer at Sotsu, Inc. in Tokyo, Japan. He has been programming professionally in a variety of languages for over 5 years now, and programming has been his hobby since he was 10 years old. He specializes in multiplatform mobile deployment, but he has experience in developing games for single platforms as well. His first mobile game was developed using the Sparrow engine. He was also featured in the book *Mobile Game Engines: Interviews with Mobile Game Engine Developers*, *Jason Brownlee*, *LuLu Press*, where he talks more about his experience with Sparrow. His talent is not limited to mobile development though. In his final year of college, he helped develop a 3D prototype game, utilizing a brain-computer interface as one of the game's inputs. He hopes to excel in and enjoy his profession, no matter how it changes.

Alex Harrison is a mobile game programmer, originally from the UK. He first learned to code with Flash and ActionScript before migrating to mobile with Sparrow and eventually Starling. He is currently working on a multiplatform project in C++ and JavaScript using cocos2DX, and he develops casual mobile browser games in his spare time. Alex lives in Cape Town, South Africa, with his wife, two kids, two dogs, two rabbits, three cats, several chickens, a horse, and a pony.

Karuna Krishnasamy is an avid gamer and a recent graduate in Computer Gaming and Animation Technology from Anglia Ruskin University. With 5 years of experience in designing and building games for the PC and iOS devices, he enjoys the process of putting a game together as much as he enjoys playing the finished product. When he isn't scoring kills in *Battlefield 4* or trying to think of the next big game idea, you can find him on the paintball field, which in his words, is the best form of exercise. You can check out some of his work at http://karunaskj.com/.

I would like to thank Johannes Stein for writing an awesome, well-written, and comprehensive beginner's guide for Sparrow. It's definitely one of my favorite frameworks, and if I had this book when I started getting into Sparrow, it definitely would have speeded up my development. I would also like to thank my family for supporting my desire to study game design and for being there to support me through many sleepless nights getting my first iOS games out in the market. Finally, I want to thank my first boss, Deepak Setty, for being an awesome mentor and role model, showing me the ins and outs of the corporate world; he is someone whom I have the utmost respect for.

Daniel Sperl is a long-time game developer and has created numerous casual games in ActionScript, C#, and Objective-C. Unsatisfied with the existing 2D frameworks of the time, he created the Sparrow Framework for iOS, mimicking the tried and tested Flash API in Objective-C. Ironically, Adobe was looking for exactly such a framework for Flash when they introduced Stage3D in 2011, and so the Starling Framework was born. In 2012, he co-founded the company Gamua to be able to work full-time on his frameworks.

When he is not developing Sparrow or giving support in the forum, Daniel loves to play the latest *Zelda* or *Super Mario* game with his wife or ride his bike along the countryside of Austria. He loves birds, just like his cat.

Sladjan Trajkovic is a software engineer with a passion for game development. He has a Master's degree in Computer Science and has been working in the software industry since 2007, where he began his career as a .NET consultant.

Nowadays, he works exclusively with the iOS platform and has been involved in several big-name applications. He has also released two games, *Alien Defense Zone* and *Super Kicks*, on the App Store as an independent developer. Currently, he is working on several new projects, both games and regular applications.

Follow him on twitter at `https://twitter.com/SladanTrajkovic`.

www.PacktPub.com

Support files, eBooks, discount offers, and more

You might want to visit www.PacktPub.com for support files and downloads related to your book.

Did you know that Packt offers eBook versions of every book published, with PDF and ePub files available? You can upgrade to the eBook version at www.PacktPub.com and as a print book customer, you are entitled to a discount on the eBook copy. Get in touch with us at service@packtpub.com for more details.

At www.PacktPub.com, you can also read a collection of free technical articles, sign up for a range of free newsletters and receive exclusive discounts and offers on Packt books and eBooks.

http://PacktLib.PacktPub.com

Do you need instant solutions to your IT questions? PacktLib is Packt's online digital book library. Here, you can access, read and search across Packt's entire library of books.

Why subscribe?

- Fully searchable across every book published by Packt
- Copy and paste, print and bookmark content
- On demand and accessible via web browser

Free access for Packt account holders

If you have an account with Packt at www.PacktPub.com, you can use this to access PacktLib today and view nine entirely free books. Simply use your login credentials for immediate access.

Table of Contents

Preface

Game development is probably one of the hardest and most rewarding challenges in software development. If we are to start completely from scratch, it will take a very long time to see any results.

With the introduction of the iPhone in 2007 and subsequent devices in the following years, developing applications for mobile devices took off, and more than 1,000,000 apps can now be downloaded from the App Store.

Luckily, Sparrow, an open source game framework for iOS, provides us with a number of predefined classes and methods that will help in our game development process.

Instead of showing how to develop a part of a game example-by-example during the course of the book, we will learn each stage of game development. With each chapter, our game will mature from being just an idea to a complete entity, while extending our knowledge of Sparrow.

What this book covers

Chapter 1, Getting Started with Sparrow, shows us how to set up Xcode, Sparrow, and our game template that we will use throughout the book. This chapter also sets up our goals and expectations for the kind of game we will develop.

Chapter 2, Displaying Our First Objects, explains the concept of display objects, which we need to achieve in order to get anything to show up on the screen, and how to manipulate these objects.

Chapter 3, Managing Assets and Scenes, introduces us to the concepts of scene and asset management and how to implement them for our purposes.

Chapter 4, The Basics of Our Game, deals with setting up our game to work on iPhone, iPod Touch, and iPad in the same manner. We will also create the game skeleton in this chapter.

Chapter 5, Beautifying Our Game, covers moving and animating our entities on the screen. We will also learn how to generate sprite sheets, what to consider when using sprite sheets, and how to integrate them into our game.

Chapter 6, Adding Game Logic, focuses on getting actual gameplay into our game as well as managing our game-relevant data in separate files.

Chapter 7, User Interface, shows us how to implement the user interface in our game, for example, displaying text on the screen, structuring our user interface, and updating the user interface to what is currently happening in the game.

Chapter 8, Artificial Intelligence and Game Progression, explains what we need to know in order to implement basic artificial intelligence and how we need to apply this for our enemies in the game.

Chapter 9, Adding Audio to Our Game, covers loading audio and how to integrate them in our game.

Chapter 10, Polishing Our Game, deals with adding the last 10 percent to our game. We are going to add a main menu, an intro, and tutorial mechanics for a smoother game experience.

Chapter 11, Integrating Third-party Services, takes a look at how we could integrate third-party services such as Apple Game Center in the hope of improving our players' experience.

What you need for this book

In order to develop applications for iOS, you need to have a Mac and, preferably, the latest version of Mac OS X. Although an Apple developer account and iOS Developer Program are not necessary, it is recommended as it allows you to run the examples on actual devices such as the iPod Touch, iPhone, and iPad and distribute your applications to the Apple App Store. Keep in mind that the iOS Developer Program comes with additional costs.

There is no need to have Sparrow and Xcode installed on your system; we will cover the installation process in the first chapter.

Who this book is for

This book is intended for those who are interested in game development, those who have already dabbled in game development but haven't made any games for mobiles yet, and those who wish to publish a game on the Apple App Store in the future.

You need a solid understanding of Objective-C to follow the examples in the book, and some experience in game development is definitely helpful, although is not necessarily required.

Conventions

In this book, you will find several headings appearing frequently.

To give clear instructions of how to complete a procedure or task, we use:

Time for action – heading

1. Action 1
2. Action 2
3. Action 3

Instructions often need some extra explanation so that they make sense, so they are followed with:

What just happened?

This heading explains the working of tasks or instructions that you have just completed.

You will also find some other learning aids in the book, including:

Pop quiz – heading

These are short, multiple-choice questions intended to help you test your own understanding.

Have a go hero – heading

These practical challenges give you ideas for experimenting with what you have learned.

You will also find a number of styles of text that distinguish between different kinds of information. Here are some examples of these styles, and an explanation of their meaning.

Code words in text, database table names, folder names, filenames, file extensions, pathnames, dummy URLs, user input, and Twitter handles are shown as follows: "This class needs to be inherited from the `SPSprite` class."

A block of code is set as follows:

```
// Setting the background
SPSprite *background = [[SPSprite alloc] init];
[self addChild:background];

// Loading the logo image and bind it on the background sprite
SPSprite *logo = [SPImage imageWithContentsOfFile:@"logo.png"];
[background addChild:logo];
```

When we wish to draw your attention to a particular part of a code block, the relevant lines or items are set in bold:

```
// Setting the background
SPSprite *background = [[SPSprite alloc] init];
[self addChild:background];

// Loading the logo image and bind it on the background sprite
SPSprite *logo = [SPImage imageWithContentsOfFile:@"logo.png"];
[background addChild:logo];
```

Any command-line input or output is written as follows:

```
sudo gem install cocoapods
pod setup
touch Podfile
pod install
```

New terms and **Important words** are shown in bold. Words that you see on the screen, in menus or dialog boxes for example, appear in the text like this: "On the **Select Destination Location** screen, click on **Next** to accept the default destination."

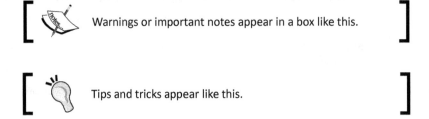

Warnings or important notes appear in a box like this.

Tips and tricks appear like this.

Reader feedback

Feedback from our readers is always welcome. Let us know what you think about this book—what you liked or may have disliked. Reader feedback is important for us to develop titles that you really get the most out of.

To send us general feedback, simply send an e-mail to `feedback@packtpub.com`, and mention the book title through the subject of your message.

If there is a topic that you have expertise in and you are interested in either writing or contributing to a book, see our author guide on `www.packtpub.com/authors`.

Customer support

Now that you are the proud owner of a Packt book, we have a number of things to help you to get the most from your purchase.

Downloading the example code

You can download the example code files for all Packt books you have purchased from your account at `http://www.packtpub.com`. If you purchased this book elsewhere, you can visit `http://www.packtpub.com/support` and register to have the files e-mailed directly to you.

Errata

Although we have taken every care to ensure the accuracy of our content, mistakes do happen. If you find a mistake in one of our books—maybe a mistake in the text or the code—we would be grateful if you would report this to us. By doing so, you can save other readers from frustration and help us improve subsequent versions of this book. If you find any errata, please report them by visiting `http://www.packtpub.com/submit-errata`, selecting your book, clicking on the **errata submission form** link, and entering the details of your errata. Once your errata are verified, your submission will be accepted and the errata will be uploaded to our website, or added to any list of existing errata, under the Errata section of that title.

Piracy

Piracy of copyright material on the Internet is an ongoing problem across all media. At Packt, we take the protection of our copyright and licenses very seriously. If you come across any illegal copies of our works, in any form, on the Internet, please provide us with the location address or website name immediately so that we can pursue a remedy.

Please contact us at copyright@packtpub.com with a link to the suspected pirated material.

We appreciate your help in protecting our authors, and our ability to bring you valuable content.

Questions

You can contact us at questions@packtpub.com if you are having a problem with any aspect of the book, and we will do our best to address it.

1
Getting Started with Sparrow

Before we dive right into the concept of development, we first need to set up our development environment and set up Sparrow on our system. In this chapter, we will take a short look at what Sparrow actually is, set up Xcode and Sparrow for our needs, create a game template, and set up goals and expectations for the game we are going to develop.

Understanding the basics of Sparrow

Sparrow is a game framework that might feel familiar to those who already have some experience with ActionScript, the Flash API, and/or Starling. The familiarity to Starling is not a coincidence; the core development team of both Starling and Sparrow are the same. Starling could be considered the ActionScript version of Sparrow. We will delve into these aspects once we use the different features of Sparrow in detail.

Open Graphics Library for Embedded Systems (OpenGL ES) is a graphics renderer for mobile devices which is available on all kinds of devices ranging from iOS devices to Android devices and even consoles such as OUYA. OpenGL can be seen as the older and bigger brother of OpenGL ES. OpenGL itself is available for all desktop platforms such as Windows, Linux, Mac OS X, and next-generation consoles such as the PlayStation 4.

OpenGL and OpenGL ES are the kind of libraries that let us perform magic on the screen, be it drawing textures, or having some kind of geometrical shapes or particle effects on the screen.

Sparrow abstracts all the OpenGL components away from the developer. We don't have to worry about the inner workings of OpenGL at all. Sparrow fully concentrates on 2D rendering and puts it into a bunch of logically structured classes and methods. While the choice for performance-heavy graphics applications is usually C or C++ as far as programming language is concerned, Sparrow uses Objective-C to keep it familiar for Mac and iOS developers.

Sparrow is not only a 2D graphics engine, but it also provides the functionality to create animations on the screen—ranging from simple effects such as fading objects in and out to more sophisticated actions such as moving a ball from the left to the right of the screen with a bouncing animation. This mechanism is also referred to as tweening.

Apart from graphic-related features, Sparrow also gives us the means to load audio files and play music and sounds in our games.

When directly compared with other game frameworks, Sparrow does not impose a specific workflow on us. As a result, a few things need to be set up by hand, such as structuring all the needed assets for our game and managing our scenes.

System requirements

From a hardware perspective, any Mac that can run the latest Mac OS X works just fine.

On the software side, we will need the latest version of Mac OS X and all the latest updates need to be installed. The minimum at the time of writing this book is OS X 10.8 Mountain Lion.

For the platforms we are going to target, we need at least a device with iOS 5.0 and Xcode 4.0 or higher. The latest version of Sparrow uses OpenGL ES 2.0 internally, which is only supported by iPhone 3GS or newer devices.

Setting up the Apple developer account

Setting up the Apple developer account and joining the iOS developer program is entirely optional for the purpose of this book, but it will become necessary if you would like to test the game on a physical device or publish it to the Apple App Store.

The iOS Simulator bundled with Apple Developer Tools is a great platform to test different functionalities. However, performance can be misleading in the simulator itself. Performance is a crucial factor in game development, so testing on a real device should be a priority.

Depending on the performance of your Mac, apps on the iOS simulator can run from terribly slow to quite fast. All in all, don't take the performance in the simulator as a reference to how well the game is going to perform on real devices.

For more information on the iOS developer program and Apple developer accounts, go to `https://developer.apple.com/`.

Downloading Xcode

Xcode is the default integrated-development environment for developing everything related to Mac and iOS. Xcode is available for free and the latest version—at the time of writing this book—is 5.0.2.

The first step is to download Xcode from the Mac App Store. Click on the Mac App Store icon from the dock to open the Mac App Store.

Search Xcode using the search box and select the appropriate result.

The store page might look something like the following screenshot:

Click on the **Install** button right under the logo. (If Xcode is already installed, the caption of the button changes to **Installed**.) The download is around 2.6 GB, so it may take a while depending on the speed of your Internet connection.

It's always a good idea to keep the Xcode installation up to date as updates are frequent.

Downloading Sparrow

Now that Xcode is installed and ready to go, the next step is to get the latest stable version of Sparrow. Go to the official Sparrow homepage at `http://sparrow-framework.org` or `http://gamua.com/sparrow/`.

The latest Sparrow version—at the time of writing this book—is 2.0.1. The download page will look like the following screenshot:

Click on the big blue **Download** button and the download should start.

Cloning the Git repository

If you are familiar with the version control system Git, you can also get the latest version by cloning the Git repository. This section is meant for advanced users who have already worked with Git.

The Sparrow GitHub repository is located at `https://github.com/Gamua/Sparrow-Framework/`, where more information on the procedure can be found. Typically, Git commands are entered in the terminal:

```
git clone https://github.com/Gamua/Sparrow-Framework
```

This will take a while to download; the current progress is being shown in the terminal. After the download is complete, you will have the latest development version. Only use this version if you want to test a specific feature of Sparrow before its release or if you are feeling adventurous.

Never use this version for production code in games about to be released on Apple's App Store.

To get the latest stable version of Sparrow, check out the stable tag:

```
git checkout tags/v2.0.1
```

Now we can update to the latest version if we want to.

Contents of the Sparrow package

After the download has finished, extract the file to a location of your choice. We can use the unpacker that is included in Mac OS X by default, but any third-party unpacker should work as well. Let's take a look at the following screenshot to see what the Sparrow package has to offer:

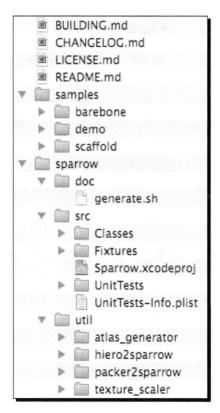

The samples folder

The `samples` folder consists of three subfolders, and they are as follows:

- ◆ `barebone`: This is a bare minimum project and a good start for creating your own games and will serve as the template for our game as well
- ◆ `demo`: This is a sample application showcasing many of the features found within Sparrow
- ◆ `scaffold`: The scaffold template provides some base classes and more boilerplate code than the `barebone` example

The sparrow folder

The `sparrow` folder has three subfolders, and they are as follows:

- ◆ `doc`: This has a script to generate the documentation
- ◆ `src`: This is the entire source of the Sparrow framework itself
- ◆ `util`: This has different command-line tools which will help our workflow when dealing with graphic assets

Markdown files in the root folder

Markdown files are, in essence, text files that can be rendered into HTML files. They are as follows:

- ◆ `BUILDING.md`: This gives a quick start on how to use the library
- ◆ `CHANGELOG.md`: This gives a detailed list of items on what exactly changed between the versions
- ◆ `LICENSE.md`: This is the license Sparrow uses
- ◆ `README.md`: This is a short introduction into what Sparrow is

License

Sparrow is a free and open source software, which means its source can be viewed and modified by anyone.

Like many other pieces of software in the Mac/iOS universe, Sparrow is licensed under an unmodified two-clause Simplified BSD license, which allows us to use Sparrow as long as the copyright notice, the list of conditions, and the disclaimer is distributed with the source or the application.

What just happened?

We copied the `barebone` Sparrow template and used it as a template for our game. We renamed all project and scheme references and ran the template in order to see if everything went ok.

The indication for everything working as expected is when there are no errors while compiling the template and a red rectangle shows up on the screen.

Option 2 – CocoaPods

CocoaPods is a dependency manager for Objective-C projects. It can handle Mac OS X and iOS dependencies alike and is similar to package managers of other systems. It can be compared to what Ruby's package manager RubyGems is to the Ruby platform or what NPM is to Node.js.

CocoaPods needs Ruby and RubyGems to run, which is nothing to worry about, as both come preinstalled on every Mac OS X machine.

Before we begin installing CocoaPods, we need to make sure that the command-line tools are installed.

Time for action – installing command-line tools

To install command-line tools, follow these steps:

1. Open a terminal.

2. Enter `xcode-select` and press *Enter* to confirm.

3. A dialog will pop up if the command-line tools are not installed yet. If a dialog does not pop up, the command-line tools are already installed and there is nothing to do here.

4. Click on the **Install** button to continue as shown in the following screenshot:

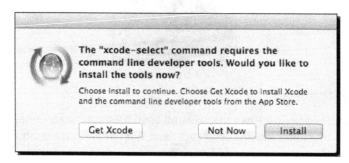

What just happened?

Before we can install CocoaPods, we need to have the latest version of the command-line tools.

If you want to trigger a reinstallation of the command-line tools regardless of whether they are already installed, this can be achieved by entering `xcode-select --install`.

Now that the command-line tools are installed, we can begin with the CocoaPods installation.

Time for action – installing CocoaPods

To install CocoaPods, follow these steps:

1. Open a terminal.

2. Enter `sudo gem update –system` and press *Enter* to confirm.

3. Enter `sudo gem install cocoapods`.

4. Enter pod setup. This may take a long time, so be patient.

```
johanness-mini:~ johannesstein$ pod setup
Setting up CocoaPods master repo
Already up-to-date.
Setup completed (read-only access)
johanness-mini:~ johannesstein$
```

What just happened?

As CocoaPods needs to be installed using the command line, our requirement is to have a terminal window opened.

In the second step, we are going to update RubyGems to the latest available version.

After that, we trigger the installation of CocoaPods. This also installs all dependencies. If there is a conflict, we get a prompt to deal with this conflict. If you are unsure about what to do, just press *Enter* in this case and the safest option will be chosen.

The last step is necessary in order to set up CocoaPods. It's recommended to run this command from time to time as it updates the local repository with all the latest specifications of libraries that can be used.

Now that CocoaPods is installed, we can go ahead and set up our Sparrow template.

Time for action – using the barebone project as a template

Follow these steps to use the barebone project as a template:

1. Copy the barebone application from **samples | barebone** to a location of your choice.

2. Open the Xcode project.

3. Click on the project name in the project navigator to make it editable.

4. Rename it to PirateGame.

5. Open the **Product** menu from the top menu bar.

6. Select **Scheme** and **Manage Schemes**.

7. Rename the **Scheme** name from **Barebone** to PirateGame.

8. Close Xcode.

9. Open any text editor.

10. Type in the following code:

```
platform :ios, '5.0'

pod 'Sparrow-Framework', '2.0.1'
```

11. Save the file as `Podfile` in the recently copied `barebone` folder on the same level as the Xcode project file. If you are using TextEdit (OS X default text editor), make sure to save the file in the plain format which can be done by changing **Format** to **Make Plain Text** in the menu. Also disable **Smart Quotes** by navigating to **TextEdit | Preferences....**

12. Open a terminal.

13. Navigate to the copied `barebone` folder.

14. Execute the `pod install` command in the terminal.

15. Open `PirateGame.xcworkspace` with Xcode.

16. Remove `Sparrow.xcodeproj` from the project by right-clicking on it and selecting **Delete**.

17. Run the project in the iOS Simulator by hitting the play button. If there are any errors, try to change the **Build Settings** in the configuration by changing **recursive** to **non-recursive** in **User Header Search Paths**.

What just happened?

We copied the barebone Sparrow template and used it as a template for our game. We renamed all project and scheme references.

We then needed to close Xcode, as CocoaPods will generate some files and we didn't want Xcode to interfere with the process.

In the next step, we had to define `Podfile`, which is the specification file for CocoaPods. This file tells CocoaPods which dependencies to fetch.

The specifications are written in Ruby, but they are easily understandable even to those who don't know the Ruby programming language.

The first statement sets the dependencies for the iOS platform. As mentioned earlier, CocoaPods can handle Mac OS and iOS dependencies even in the same project, so it makes sense for it to have a statement separating one from the other. As we are only targeting iOS, we don't need to worry about Mac OS dependencies and we leave that one out.

The second part of the `Podfile` in our example has all the dependencies we need in our project. As we only have one dependency—which is Sparrow—we only need to define that one.

A dependency is written in the following format:

```
pod 'name' 'version'
```

The repository with all dependencies and versions currently available can be found on GitHub at `https://github.com/CocoaPods/Specs`.

After our `Podfile` is written and saved, we need to get back to the terminal and let CocoaPods fetch our dependencies which is what `pod install` does. CocoaPods also generates a `Pod` folder which is where all dependencies are stored as well as an Xcode workspace.

From now on, instead of opening the project file, we need to open the workspace file as this is what CocoaPods updates and maintains.

If we were to open the project file and try to run the application, the application would fail to compile.

As the last step, we run our example. The indication that everything worked fine is when there are no errors while compiling the template and a red rectangle shows up on the screen.

Running the template on the actual device

Even though our template is still a bit basic, we can run it on an actual device. For this section, we'll need an Apple developer account and we will need to be a member of the iOS Developer Program.

Time for action – running the template on the actual device

To run the template on the actual device, follow these steps:

1. Open the Xcode settings through **Xcode** at the top menu bar and then click on **Preferences...**.

2. Navigate to **Accounts**.

3. Click on the plus icon to add a new account.

4. Select **Add Apple ID...** from the menu.

5. Enter the required credentials and confirm by clicking on **Add**.

6. Connect your device to your Mac.

7. Open the Xcode organizer by going to **Window | Organizer** to check whether the device has been successfully detected.

8. Select the device from the menu by clicking on the application name and selecting the correct device.

9. Run the project by hitting the play button.

What just happened?

We connected a device to our Mac, and set the build configuration to the device so that the application would run on the device instead of the simulator.

As expected, the red rectangle should be successfully displayed on the device as it did on the simulator.

Getting Sparrow documentation files

The Sparrow framework features documentation, also known as a docset, which can be integrated in order to get additional information on Sparrow classes and methods.

To add a docset for Xcode 5, a free application called **Docs for Xcode** is necessary and can be downloaded from the Mac App Store. More information on Docs for Xcode can be found at `http://documancer.com/xcode/`.

Time for action – adding the Sparrow API documentation to Xcode

To add the Sparrow API documentation, just follow these easy steps:

1. Open Docs for Xcode (if you launch Docs for Xcode for the first time, grant it the access to the documentation folder).

2. Click on **Add Feed**.

3. Enter `http://doc.sparrow-framework.org/core/feed/docset.atom` in the text field and confirm by clicking on **Add**.

4. Restart Xcode (or open Xcode if Xcode was already closed).

5. Open a Sparrow project and open the inline documentation by pressing the *Alt* button and clicking on any class name or method.

```
// add background image
SPImage *background = [SPImage imageWithContentsOfFile:@"background.jpg"];

Description  An SPImage displays a quad with a texture mapped onto it.

Declared in  SPImage.h

Reference  SPImage                                              ain menu

_mainMenu.y = _offsetY;
```

What just happened?

We added a docset feed in Docs for Xcode so that we get more precise and always up-to-date documentation when developing with Sparrow.

The idea for the game

Finding the right idea for a game can be quite tricky. As a rule of thumb, find something to be excited about and something you might want to play yourself. A good motivation is playing games and finding bits and pieces that you really like or that can be improved. One thing is for certain: do not clone. Don't make clones, make something original instead.

Finding game ideas

Probably the best way to find game ideas is during game jams, where you get to develop a game in a very short time frame. One of the more popular ones is Ludum Dare (`http://www.ludumdare.com/compo/`) and Global Game Jam (`http://globalgamejam.org/`). The first one is an online solo competition whereas at Global Game Jam you have to work in teams. What both game jams have in common is a theme that is provided and should be used by all entrants.

For a less competitive approach, you might also want to check the Twitter `@PeterMolydeux`, which is a parody account of Peter Molyneux, the creative mind behind Fable, Black & White, and Populous. There are tweets about completely crazy and/or funny game ideas, most of which would be very fun to play.

The kind of game we are developing is something a bit like an action game with role-playing game elements. The player is going to control a ship full of pirates who are waiting for ships to attack, seize, and scavenge.

After each mission, we'll get back to the pirate cove and buy better items such as cannonballs or hire a more experienced crew. Our game will be called "A Practical Survival Guide for Pirates". However, as the name is long, we'll just leave the game template name as "PirateGame".

Setting goals and expectations

It's always a good idea to have some kind of plan. While most of game development is iterative, it doesn't hurt to communicate the vision of the game.

The most important thing when developing is to remember the scope. It's very important to keep the scope as small as possible; in most situations, you still have to cut gameplay elements out in latter stages of the development cycle.

So saying we are going to create the next *Angry Birds* with more levels is probably as unrealistic as saying we're going to develop the next *World of WarCraft* just with more weapons and quests.

Let's put our goals and expectations into a list. The following is the list of goals we have for this book:

- Finished game by the end of the book
- Gained an understanding of development with Sparrow
- Examples are relevant for game development and working with Sparrow

The following is the list of expectations we have out of this book:

- The game is polished enough so that it can be published to the Apple App Store
- The game is fun to play

Examining our gameplay elements

Most independent games generally focus on a single mechanic and polish it to the maximum. *Tiny Wings* and *Snapshot* are good examples.

As with all software, there is always the danger of becoming a feature creep, which means adding all kinds of features during development without planning for it or balancing. In the end, the game might have all the features we want, but these features might be mutually exclusive and the game might not be fun.

So keeping in mind the scope and limitations, let's make a list with our features and gameplay elements for our game:

- Attacking enemy ships
- Collecting loot from enemy ships
- Upgrading ship equipments
- Hiring new crew members

Code conventions

Before we head into our first lines of code, we should take a moment and settle on code conventions for all code examples. The most used code guideline in the Objective-C world is the one made by Apple, which we are going to follow as closely as possible.

The most important conventions to remember are as follows:

- Keep all method names in camel case (as in `myMethodName`)
- The method names should be descriptive
- Don't abbreviate method names
- Instance variables should be prefixed with an underscore

The complete guideline for these conventions is available at `https://developer.apple.com/library/mac/documentation/Cocoa/Conceptual/CodingGuidelines/CodingGuidelines.html`.

Pop quiz

Q1. What is the Sparrow Framework?

1. A game framework for 2D games
2. A 3D graphics engine
3. A scene graph library

Q2. What is CocoaPods?

1. Source control for Objective-C
2. An add-on library for Cocoa
3. A dependency manager for Objective-C packages

Q3. In order to develop games with Sparrow 2.x, we need at least iOS 5.0 SDK and preferably an iPhone 3GS or a more recent device.

1. True
2. False

Summary

We learned a lot in this chapter about setting up our development environment for Sparrow. Specifically, we covered how to set up Xcode, the Sparrow game framework, and creating our own game template.

We also touched on some general game development topics and learned about dependency management with CocoaPods.

Now that we have a game template set up, we're ready to learn about display objects and how to use them—which is the topic of the next chapter.

2
Displaying Our First Objects

In the previous chapter, we installed and configured Xcode developer tools and also as downloaded the Sparrow framework and linked it to a sample project. We proceeded to test it in both the iOS Simulator and a real device. We also set the scope for the game we are going to develop throughout the book. However, before we get into the game development process, let's touch on some core concepts of Sparrow and get accustomed with the way things work in Sparrow. We will draw some objects on the screen and manipulate these objects by applying rotation and scaling transforms.

Understanding display objects

As the name suggests, a display object is something that will be displayed on the screen. We can think of display objects as separate graphical entities that contain different kinds of graphical data. While this may sound a bit abstract at first, every image (SPImage), quads (SPQuad), or other geometrical shapes are derived from the SPDisplayObject class, which is the representation of a display object in Sparrow.

Explaining display object containers

A display object container (`SPDisplayObjectContainer`) inherits from `SPDisplayObject`, adding the facility to own a set of child display objects. When you add a child display object to a parent display object container, you can think of it as attaching one display object to another. If you move, scale, or rotate the parent display object, all the changes are inherited by any children it might have. This concept is more or less identical to how objects on the screen are managed in the Adobe Flash API. The full set of parent and child nodes is referred to as the display list, or sometimes as a display tree. This is because, like a tree, it contains many branches that all ultimately converge into one single trunk, often referred to as the root. Yet another name for a display tree is a scene graph.

The display list draws the display objects in the order they are added to their parent display object container. If we were to add a second child display object to the same parent as that of the previously added display object, the second display object will be drawn in front of the first.

Let's go ahead and imagine ourselves as a cardboard puppet doll. We need a head, a torso and a leg, arm, and hand on the left side and the same goes for the right side. Refer to the following diagram that displays this concept:

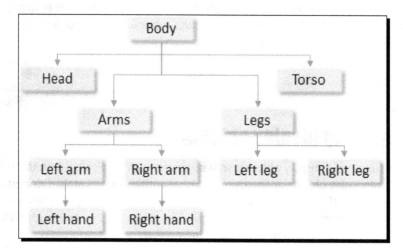

The root object for this arrangement would be the body object. The head, torso, legs, and arms would be directly bound to the body and the hands would be bound to each arm.

Setting the background color

Before we draw a couple of objects on the screen, let's change the background color of our application that will eventually become our game.

Time for action – changing the background color

Let's take a look at the required steps to change the background color:

1. Open our Xcode game template if it's not already open.

2. Open the Game.m source file.

3. After the initialization method and before the existing SPQuad object, add the following lines:

```
SPQuad *background = [SPQuad quadWithWidth:Sparrow.stage.width
    height:Sparrow.stage.height color:0xffffff];
[self addChild:background];
```

4. Run the example.

When the example is running, we see our red rectangle on a white background as shown in the following screenshot:

What just happened?

In step 1, we opened our Xcode template that we created in the previous chapter, and in step 2, we navigated to the Game.m file, which is where our game code currently lies. The game is the red rectangle that keeps showing up.

In step 3, right before we drew our red rectangle, we defined the background variable that is a pointer to an instance of SPQuad. The SPQuad class is derived from SPDisplayObject. The function of SPQuad is to draw a rectangular shape with a background color.

The SPQuad class provides a few factory methods for operations such as creating a quad with a width and height and also adds a color value to it. In this example, we are creating a quad with a predefined width and height and a color value of 0xffffff. A color is defined as 0xRRGGBB in a hexadecimal notation, that is, REDRED GREENGREEN BLUEBLUE.

While at the surface, the call to [SPQuad quadWithWidth:Sparrow.stage.width height:Sparrow.stage.height] seems to be the same as the one to [[SPQuad alloc] initWithWidth:Sparrow.stage.width height:Sparrow.stage.height], but there is one major difference under the hood. When the factory method is called, it returns an auto-released object, which means we don't have an ownership over the instance and it's being destroyed at some point. On the other hand, if we use the alloc-and-init combination, we do have the ownership and the need to release the instance ourselves.

As our application uses **Automatic Reference Counting (ARC)**, we don't need to worry about releasing instances ourselves. On the other hand, Sparrow itself uses **Manual Reference Counting (MRC)**.

To cover the whole screen, we need to get the width and height of the screen itself. Those values are available as properties in the Sparrow.stage object.

We need to add the background to the Game class, which is exactly what [self addChild:background] does. The self keyword is a reference to the Game class, which is derived from the SPSprite class.

Now, we have a white background with a red rectangle that appears on top of it.

Our Game.m source file should contain the following code:

```
#import "Game.h"

@implementation Game

- (id)init
{
    if ((self = [super init]))
    {
        SPQuad *background = [SPQuad
          quadWithWidth:Sparrow.stage.width
            height:Sparrow.stage.height color:0xffffff];
        [self addChild:background];

        SPQuad *quad = [SPQuad quadWithWidth:100 height:100];
        quad.color = 0xff0000;
        quad.x = 50;
        quad.y = 50;
        [self addChild:quad];
```

```
    }
    return self;
}

@end
```

There is also an easier way to set the background color. While the performance penalty in
this specific case is not that high to worry about, we could directly set the color through
Sparrow.stage by using its color property: Sparrow.stage.color = 0xffffff. It
consists of fewer lines, is more readable, and shows its intention better.

What is a stage?

We briefly touched on the topic of Sparrow.stage, which so far proved to have some
useful properties for getting the width and height of the screen and setting the background
color directly.

A stage is the top-level element of any Sparrow game and logically the root element of the
display tree, which Sparrow automatically creates for us.

Creating our cardboard puppet doll

Let's implement the cardboard puppet doll that we talked about in the beginning of the
chapter. Remove the red rectangle that has been drawn on the screen.

Time for action – creating a cardboard puppet doll

To create the cardboard puppet doll, we need to perform the following steps:

1. Open the Game.m file if it's not already open.

2. Add a body container with the following lines:

```
SPSprite *body = [[SPSprite alloc] init];
body.x = 85;
body.y = 120;

[self addChild:body];
```

3. Add `torso` as shown in the following code:

```
SPQuad *torso = [SPQuad quadWithWidth:150 height:150];
torso.color = 0xff0000;

[body addChild:torso];
```

4. Now add a local variable `head` as shown in the following code:

```
SPQuad *head = [SPQuad quadWithWidth:80 height:80
   color:SP_YELLOW];
head.x = 35;
head.y = -70;

[body addChild: head];
```

5. Add a container for the `arms` local variable as shown in the following code:

```
SPSprite *arms = [[SPSprite alloc] init];

[body addChild:arms];
```

6. Add a container for the `legs` local variable as shown in the following code:

```
SPSprite *legs = [[SPSprite alloc] init];
legs.y = 140;

[body addChild:legs];
```

7. Add the left arm as shown in the following code:

```
SPQuad *leftArm = [SPQuad quadWithWidth:100 height:50
   color:0x00ff00];
leftArm.x = -80;

[arms addChild:leftArm];
```

8. Add the right arm as shown in the following code:

```
SPQuad *rightArm = [SPQuad quadWithWidth:100 height:50
   color:0x00ff00];
rightArm.x = 130;

[arms addChild:rightArm];
```

9. Every arm needs a hand. Let's add the left one first as shown in the following code:

```
SPQuad *leftHand = [SPQuad quadWithWidth:40 height:50
   color:SP_YELLOW];
leftHand.x = -80;

[arms addChild:leftHand];
```

10. Now use the following code for the right hand:

```
SPQuad *rightHand = [SPQuad quadWithWidth:40 height:50
  color:SP_YELLOW];
rightHand.x = 190;

[arms addChild:rightHand];
```

11. Let's move on to the legs. We'll create the left one first with the following code:

```
SPQuad *leftLeg = [SPQuad quadWithWidth:50 height:150
  color:0x0000ff];

[legs addChild:leftLeg];
```

12. We'll create the right leg with the following code:

```
SPQuad *rightLeg = [SPQuad quadWithWidth:50 height:150
  color:0x0000ff];
rightLeg.x = 100;

[legs addChild:rightLeg];
```

13. Run the example.

When we run the example, a simple cardboard puppet doll made of rectangles is looking right at us, as shown in the following screenshot:

What just happened?

In step 1, we used the Game.m source file we are already familiar with.

At first, we needed a container object, which we called body for this example. A quad would not suffice in this case because SPQuad does not inherit from SPDisplayObjectContainer and so cannot have children added to it. We set the x and y properties, so the contents of the body element appeared somewhere in the middle of our screen. The coordinate system in Sparrow started at the top-left corner of the screen, just like how the coordinate system works in Flash or in traditional application development when adding control elements to a window. Developers from a traditional graphics development may take some time to get used to this. In OpenGL, for example, the *y* axis is flipped. We then add the body element to our Game instance.

In step 3, we took the torso, which is a quad and added it to the body element. If we don't specify an x or y property, their default value is 0.

After that, we added the head. The x and y properties are measured relative to the parent display object. So, if we use a negative value, it doesn't necessarily mean that the element is drawn outside the screen. It depends on the position of the parent display object container.

While we know that we can use colors with the hexadecimal notation, we are using SP_YELLOW in this step. This has the same effect as typing 0xffff00.

For the arms and legs, we added a container for each in step 5 and step 6, respectively. SPSprite is the most basic and lightweight container class that should be used when grouping objects. The leg container is already being positioned a bit to the bottom, so its children elements only need to be positioned horizontally.

In the remaining steps, we added each limb and when we finally ran the application, we had a cardboard puppet doll made of rectangles looking at us.

Have a go hero – improving the cardboard puppet doll

Our code can be improved quite a bit; the legs, arms, and hands code are practically the same, but we define each element separately. We could try to group and simplify the code a bit.

Also, in the current arrangement, the hands are not directly connected to the arms of the doll. Instead, they are bound to the arms container object. So if we were to move a single arm, the hand would not move with the arm.

The following are some ideas on how to solve these problems:

- In order to connect the hands to the arms, we would need at least two new container objects
- Make a cardboard puppet doll class in which its elements are classes inheriting from the display object containers

Explaining macros

While we know that we can use colors with the hexadecimal notation, Sparrow provides some shorthand constants for the most commonly used colors. In the previous example, instead of using `0xffff00` for the color yellow, we used `SP_YELLOW`.

To generalize, macros are handy little functions that allow us to simplify the workflow when working with repetitious tasks.

Macros in Objective-C are preprocessor directives and work the same way that macros work in C and C++. Before the code is compiled, the preprocessor goes through the entire code and replaces all occurrences of the macro with the result of the macro.

While we could write each color in the hexadecimal color value notation, sometimes it does make more sense to use an RGB value. The `SP_COLOR` macro does exactly that, converting a RGB color into a hexadecimal color value.

In this section, we will look at what the different kinds of macros are and how to use them.

The Angles macro

Sparrow uses radians to describe the rotation of its display objects. If we want to use degrees for our calculations, we would need the following macros:

Name	Description	Example
SP_R2D	Converts radians to degrees	SP_R2D(PI);
		// 180
SP_D2R	Converts degrees to radians	SP_D2R(180);
		// PI

The Colors macro

If we need to create a custom color or take an existing color apart, the following macros would fit our purpose:

Name	Description	Example
SP_COLOR_PART_ALPHA SP_COLOR_PART_RED SP_COLOR_PART_GREEN SP_COLOR_PART_BLUE	Getting the partial value of a color	SP_COLOR_PART_RED(0xff0000); // 0xff
SP_COLOR	Sets an RGB color	SP_COLOR(255, 255, 0); // 0xffff00
SP_COLOR_ARGB	Sets an ARGB color	SP_COLOR_ARGB(128, 255, 255, 0); // 0x80ffff00

The utility functions

Let's take a look at the last group of macros that aren't angle- or color-related:

Name	Description	Example
SP_IS_FLOAT_EQUAL	Does a float comparison between two values. Returns 0 if it's false, 1 if it's true.	SP_IS_FLOAT_EQUAL(0.11, 0.12); // 0
SP_CLAMP	Clamps between two values. The first parameter is the initial value. The other two parameters are the minimum and maximum values respectively.	SP_CLAMP(0.6, 1.0, 2.0); // 1.0
SP_SWAP	Swaps two values with each other.	NSUInteger x = 0; NSUInteger y = 1; SP_SWAP(x, y, NSUInteger); // x = 1; y = 0

Constants in Sparrow

We already know about SP_YELLOW, so let's take a look at what constants are defined in Sparrow.

Math

The `PI` constant, for example, is used in the macro to convert radians to degrees and vice versa. The following are the examples of `PI` constant:

Name	Description
PI	The value of Pi
PI_HALF	The value of Pi divided by two
TWO_PI	The value of Pi multiplied by two

Color

Sparrow predefines 16 colors for easier usage, so we don't have to use a macro each time. These are the most basic colors and are also defined in a number of different libraries and frameworks, for example, HTML 4.01. The following table shows 16 colors that are predefined in Sparrow:

Name	RGB value	Hex value
SP_WHITE	255, 255, 255	0xffffff
SP_SILVER	208, 208, 208	0xc0c0c0
SP_GRAY	128, 128, 128	0x808080
SP_BLACK	0, 0, 0	0x000000
SP_RED	255, 0, 0	0xff0000
SP_MAROON	128, 0, 0	0x800000
SP_YELLOW	255, 255, 0	0xffff00
SP_OLIVE	128, 128, 0	0x808000
SP_LIME	0, 255, 0	0x00ff00
SP_GREEN	0, 128, 0	0x008000
SP_AQUA	0, 255, 255	0x00ffff
SP_TEAL	0, 128, 128	0x008080
SP_BLUE	0, 0, 255	0x0000ff
SP_NAVY	0, 0, 128	0x000080
SP_FUCHSIA	255, 0, 255	0xff00ff
SP_PURPLE	128, 0, 128	0x800080

Manipulating display objects

Now that we have our cardboard puppet doll on the screen, let's start manipulating the objects on the screen.

In this example, we will take a look at how to rotate, scale, and skew objects, and then set the origin of these objects.

Time for action – manipulating display objects

Perform the following steps to manipulate the display objects we created earlier:

1. Add a new method to Game.m below the init method we used to create the body parts:

```
- (void)onLegTouch:(SPTouchEvent *)event
{
  SPTouch *touch = [[event touchesWithTarget:self
    andPhase:SPTouchPhaseBegan] anyObject];
  if (touch) {
    SPQuad* target = (SPQuad *) event.target;

    float currentRotation = SP_R2D(target.rotation);
    currentRoration = currentRotation + 10;

    if (currentRotation >= 360.0)
    {
      currentRotation = currentRotation - 360.0;
    }
    target.rotation = SP_D2R(currentRotation);
  }
}
```

2. Next, we'll need to set the anchor (pivot) of our legs in the initializer, as shown in the following code:

```
leftLeg.pivotX = 25;
leftLeg.pivotY = 10;

rightLeg.pivotX = 25;
rightLeg.pivotY = 10;
```

3. Update the leg positions using the following code:

```
SPQuad *leftLeg = [SPQuad quadWithWidth:50 height:150
  color:0x0000ff];
[legs addChild:leftLeg];
leftLeg.x = 25;

SPQuad *rightLeg = [SPQuad quadWithWidth:50 height:150
  color:0x0000ff];
rightLeg.x = 125;
[legs addChild:rightLeg];
```

4. We'll set an event listener for the legs using the following code:

```
[rightLeg addEventListener:@selector(onLegTouch:) atObject:self
  forType:SP_EVENT_TYPE_TOUCH];
[leftLeg addEventListener:@selector(onLegTouch:) atObject:self
  forType:SP_EVENT_TYPE_TOUCH];
```

5. Let's add another method that should be called when we touch the head of our cardboard puppet doll. This method should be below the initializer and the onLegTouch method:

```
- (void)onHeadTouch:(SPTouchEvent *)event
{
    SPTouch *touch = [[event touchesWithTarget:self
      andPhase:SPTouchPhaseBegan] anyObject];
    if (touch) {
        SPQuad* target = (SPQuad *) event.target;
        target.scaleX = (target.scaleX == 1.0) ? 1.5 : 1.0;
        target.scaleY = (target.scaleY == 1.0) ? 1.5 : 1.0;
    }
}
```

6. We'll need to set the pivot for the head as well:

```
head.pivotX = head.width / 2;
head.pivotY = head.height / 2;
```

7. Let's update the position of the head as shown in the following code:

```
SPQuad *head = [SPQuad quadWithWidth:80 height:80
  color:SP_YELLOW];
head.x = 75;
head.y = -30;
[body addChild: head];
```

8. Let's add an event listener for the head as shown in the following code:

```
[head addEventListener:@selector(onHeadTouch:) atObject:self
  forType:SP_EVENT_TYPE_TOUCH];
```

9. Add another method that should be called if we touch the arms. This is shown in the following code:

```
- (void)onArmsTouch:(SPTouchEvent *)event
{
    SPTouch *touch = [[event touchesWithTarget:self
      andPhase:SPTouchPhaseBegan] anyObject];
    if (touch) {
        SPQuad* target = (SPQuad *) event.target;
```

```
      target.skewX = (target.skewX == SP_D2R(20)) ? SP_D2R(0)
         : SP_D2R(20);
      target.skewY = (target.skewY == SP_D2R(20)) ? SP_D2R(0)
         : SP_D2R(20);
   }
}
```

10. Bind the event listener to this newly added method:

```
[arms addEventListener:@selector(onArmsTouch:) atObject:self
   forType:SP_EVENT_TYPE_TOUCH];
```

11. Run the example and touch some limbs of our cardboard puppet doll. We should now see our cardboard puppet doll on the screen and if we touch an arm, leg, or the head, we see these objects rotated, skewed, or scaled.

What just happened?

In step 1, we defined a method that should be called when we touch one of the legs. We need to get a reference to the touch event, which in Sparrow is described as SPTouchEvent. To get the touch instance (SPTouch), we looked for touches on any object in the touch began phase. Each touch moves through three phases: first SPTouchPhaseBegan, then SPTouchPhaseMoved, and finally SPTouchPhaseEnded. We need to check whether the touch is valid as objects have been touched by using it as a condition in the if-statement. The current target of the event is available in event.target although it needs to be casted to the appropriate display object type, in this case, SPQuad.

We then got the current rotation of the touched object and add 10 degrees to the rotation. The new rotation will be set to the quad. If the rotation is bigger than 360 degrees, we'll subtract 360 degrees.

The origin for display objects is, by default, the top-left corner of the display object itself. If we want a different origin, we'll need to modify it using the `pivotX` and `pivotY` properties of a display object.

Modifying the origin also has an effect on the positioning of the element; so, if we want to keep the same position, we need to add the pivot value to the position values, which is what happened in step 3.

In step 4, we added an event listener for each of the legs, so when we actually touch the legs, something happens. When using `addEventListener`, we are binding a selector that will be called once the event is triggered, in our case, `SP_EVENT_TYPE_TOUCH`. This event will be called if any touch occurs on the specified object, which was `self` (the `Game` instance) in this step. Multiple selectors can be bound to one event when using `addEventListener` each time.

For the next step, we added a method for touching the head of our cardboard puppet doll. We also needed to do the same touch check and target casting we did last time. This time when we touch the head, it should scale up to 150 percent of its original size, and if we touch the head again, it'll shrink back to its original size.

In step 6, we set the origin to the center of the element. In step 7, we needed to update the position accordingly, and in step 8, we bound the method to the `head` element.

The last method that we defined is what would happen when we touch any `arms` element. If we are binding a touch event to a `SPSprite` instance, it will fire for all its children as well. The same touch check applies to this method. We'll skew an element by 20 degrees with the first touch and reset it to its original state when the element is touched again.

We use a ternary statement here to check whether the target is already skewed. We check for the condition within the parenthesis. If the condition evaluates against `true`, the statement after the question mark will be executed; otherwise, the statement after the colon will be executed. The advantage is that the ternary statement is an expression and can be assigned to a value in a single step. It would translate to the following code if we were to use `if` statements instead:

```
if (target.skewX == SP_D2R(20)) {
  target.skewX = SP_D2R(0);
} else {
  target.skewX = SP_D2R(20);
}

if (target.skewY == SP_D2R(20)) {
```

```
        target.skewY = SP_D2R(0);
    } else {
        target.skewY = SP_D2R(20);
    }
```

The onArmsTouch method was then bound to the arms object in step 10.

When we run the example and touch various elements, we'll see all the skewing, scaling, and rotating in action.

Pop quiz

Q1. What is an alternate term for display list/tree?

1. Display block
2. Display object
3. Scene graph

Q2. What is a Sparrow stage?

1. A game level
2. Root element of the display tree
3. A display object on the Game class

Q3. What are macros?

1. Functions that are evaluated at runtime
2. Preprocessor directives that are evaluated before compiling
3. Dynamic constants

Summary

We learned a lot in this chapter about how to display objects on the screen and how to manipulate them.

Specifically, we covered how to display objects on the screen and use macros and constants Sparrow provides. Another important aspect is that we manipulated the objects we drew on the screen.

We also touched on some topics such as the Sparrow stage and got an overview of how the Sparrow API works.

Now that we know how to draw objects on the screen, we're ready to learn about asset and scene management—which is the topic of the next chapter.

3
Managing Assets and Scenes

In the previous chapter, we drew our first display objects on the screen, which in our case were quads. We made a cardboard puppet doll out of quads and learned how to use macros. There is one last thing we need to know before developing our pirate game. In this chapter, we will learn about managing our assets, such as images, sound, and other kinds of files. We will also learn how to group elements into scenes and display these scenes.

Working with assets

When we develop a game, we load files. We probably load a lot of images too. These images are displayed on the screen and are the graphics of any 2D game.

We will also need to load sound files for playing music and sound effects. Other general purpose files include text files that are either localization or game information files, such as hit points for enemies, attack strength, or similar data that affects the gameplay of the game.

Game-relevant data may include saved games and level data. This gameplay-relevant data may not always be plain text; in some cases, they are binary files or they use a markup language such as XML or JSON. In the iOS and Mac world, the PLIST file format is very common and contains a specialized kind of XML format.

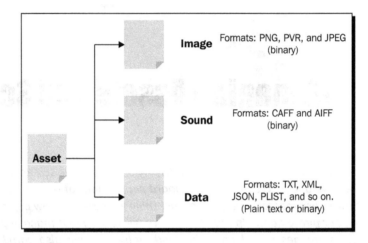

In some games, game engines and game frameworks go a step further when dealing with gameplay-relevant data in order to be more dynamic. They allow scripting through languages such as Lua and JavaScript. These scripts are loaded and executed at runtime.

Managing our assets

Now that we know what assets are, how can we manage them for our game? Before we get to that, let's take a look at what we know so far and what the prerequisites to effectively load assets are.

Firstly, we know that there are different kinds of assets that can either be plain text files or binary.

One thing to keep in mind is the memory in mobile devices nowadays. While it is the same as the memory in desktop devices from a few years back, not all of this is reserved for our application. We should also keep in mind that the size of an asset on the disk may not be the same in memory as it is for compressed files, especially if the file content is compressed on the disk but has to be uncompressed in memory.

Consequently, there are a few things we can do, which are as follows:

- Limit the number of assets we are loading; this can prove difficult as a game can require a high amount of assets
- Limit the number of assets that are currently loaded in memory
- Cache assets that are already loaded so that we don't have the same content in memory two or more times

Let's create a base class that manages a group of assets.

Time for action – creating a base class

To create a base class to manage our assets, we need to use the following steps:

1. Open the Xcode game template if it's not already open, right-click on the **Classes** folder, select **New Group**, and rename the group to **Assets**.

2. Right-click on the **Assets** group and select **New File...**.

3. Select **Objective-C class** and click on **Next**.

4. Enter `AssetsDictionary` in the name field, select **NSObject** from the **Subclass of** entry, and click on **Next**.

5. On the next dialog, click on **Create**.

6. Open the `AssetsDictionary.h` file.

7. Add an instance variable called `_dict`, which is a pointer to `NSMutableDictionary`, as shown in the following code:

```
@interface AssetsDictionary : NSObject {
    NSMutableDictionary *_dict;
}
```

8. Add a property called `verbose`, which is of type `BOOL`, as shown in the following code:

```
@property BOOL verbose;
```

9. Add an instance method called `registerAsset`, as shown in the following code:

```
-(id) registerAsset:(NSString *)name withContent:(id)content;
```

10. Add another instance method called `unregisterAsset`, as shown in the following code:

```
-(void) unregisterAsset:(NSString *)name;
```

11. Add a third instance method called `clear`, as shown in the following code:

```
-(void) clear;
```

12. Now switch to `AssetsDictionary.m`.

13. Add an initializer with the following content:

```
- (id) init
{
    if ((self = [super init])) {
        _dict = [[NSMutableDictionary alloc] init];
        _verbose = NO;
    }

    return self;
}
```

14. Implement the `registerAsset` method with the following piece of code:

```
-(id) registerAsset:(NSString *)name withContent:(id)content
{
  id result;

  if ([_dict objectForKey:name] == nil) {
    [_dict setObject:content forKey:name];

    result = content;

    if (self.verbose) {
      NSLog(@"Asset %@ does not exist. Registering.", name);
    }
  } else {
    result = [_dict objectForKey:name];

    if (self.verbose) {
      NSLog(@"Asset %@ already exists. Using cached value.",
        name);
    }
  }

  return result;
}
```

15. Implement the `unregisterAsset` method:

```
-(void) unregisterAsset:(NSString *)name
{
    if ([_dict objectForKey:name] != nil) {
        [_dict removeObjectForKey:name];
    }
}
```

16. Implement the `clear` method that should reset the cache:

```
-(void) clear
{
    [_dict removeAllObjects];
}
```

17. Switch to the `Game.m` file.

18. Import the `AssetsDictionary.h` file in the `import` section:

```
#import "AssetsDictionary.h"
```

19. In the `init` method, add the following lines:

```
AssetsDictionary* assets = [[AssetsDictionary alloc] init];
assets.verbose = YES;
[assets registerAsset:@"myAsset" withContent:@"test"];
[assets registerAsset:@"myAsset" withContent:@"test"];
```

20. Run the example, and you will get the following output:

```
PirateGame[4885:907] Asset myAsset does not exist. Registering.
PirateGame[4885:907] Asset myAsset already exists. Using cached value.
```

What just happened?

In step 1, we opened our Xcode template from where we left off in the previous chapter. Then, we created a new group where we put everything that relates to the management of our assets. Finally, we renamed the newly created group.

In step 2, we created a new file. In step 3, we selected **Objective-C class** from the dialog that popped up. We wanted the class name to be `AssetsDictionary`, which is what we entered in step 4; we also confirmed the location where it is going to be saved on the hard drive in step 5.

Next, we opened the header file and an instance variable to store the name and content of an asset. For this, we needed it to be an instance of NSMutableDictionary. Objective-C Cocoa classes such as NSDictionary can be mutable or immutable; the contents of mutable classes can change, and the values of immutable classes are fixed to the values used when declaring the object.

Though we put the interface section in the header, it is also possible to put it right before the implementation section.

In step 8, we added a property called verbose, which is of type BOOL. If this property is set to YES, once an asset is registered, it should write a message telling us whether the asset is already in cache. It is sufficient to say that its default value should be NO so that our console message box is not cluttered with messages.

We needed to define our method that handles the registering and serving of our assets. It takes two parameters: the name of an asset and the content of an asset. It returns the content of the asset. Since the content of the asset can be anything—but is in most cases an instance of some sort—the type id seems like the best option here. The type id can stand for any class instance; if put to a technical term, it's called dynamic typing.

Then, we defined two methods; the first explains how to delete a single asset from the cache (step 10), and the second method explains how to clear all assets (step 11).

Our header file is done; now, let's get to the actual implementation. First off, switch to the AssetsDictionary.m file. In step 13, we added an initializer, which does the following two things for us:

- Set up the _dict dictionary.
- Set the verbose property to NO by using its instance variable _verbose. This is generally not needed as NO is the default value for BOOL.

In the next step, we implemented the registerAsset method. If the key—our first parameter—does not exist in the dictionary, we add it to the dictionary and return the content of the asset. If it exists, we look up the value from the dictionary and return it. In both cases, if the verbose property is set to YES, we will print a fitting message to reflect the current state of the asset.

In step 15, we defined a method that allows us to delete a single asset from the cache. In step 16 on the other hand, we defined a method to clear the complete cache.

Now that the AssetsDictionary class is ready for action, let's put it up for a test. In step 17, we switched to our Game.m file and subsequently imported the AssetsDictionary header in step 18.

Next, within the initializer of our `Game` class, we defined an instance of our `AssetsDictionary` class, set the `verbose` property to `YES`, and registered the same asset twice to see whether it will be cached correctly. In the last step, we ran the example and looked at the output in the console.

Have a go hero

While this class works for our purposes, we could improve the `AssetsDictionary` class further. Here are some suggestions:

- When getting the cached value of an asset, we look for the value from the dictionary twice: the first time when checking whether the key is in the dictionary, and the second time when getting the actual value. This may result in a performance penalty when loading the assets into the game if there is a huge amount of assets.

- Try to use `NSCache` instead of `NSMutableDictionary`.

- If we want to display progress bars to see how far the loading process currently is, we will need a way to get the number of currently registered assets.

- We can also have an `exists` method that checks whether an asset has already been registered and returns the result of this check.

- We can add more initializers that take `NSDictionary`, for example.

Creating a texture manager

When we load an image in Sparrow, we typically want it to be a texture. A texture is pixel information that makes up an image. It's conceptually similar to how the `BitmapData` class works in ActionScript 3. If we want it to be displayed on the screen, it needs to be put on a geometrical representation, which is typically a quad.

The way we want our texture manager to work is to pass in a filename, which will be converted to a texture and is then available to us.

Let's use `AssetsDictionary` for our texture manager.

Time for action – managing our textures

To create our texture manager, take a look at the following steps:

1. Add a new Objective-C class called `TextureManager` derived from `AssetsDictionary` within the **Assets** group.

2. Add an instance method that will register a texture using its filename and return the correct value, which is the following:

```
-(SPTexture *) registerTexture:(NSString *)filename;
```

3. Switch to `TextureManager.m` and implement the method with the following content:

```
-(SPTexture *) registerTexture:(NSString *)filename
{
    if ([_dict objectForKey:filename] == nil) {
    return (SPTexture *) [self registerAsset:filename
      withContent:[SPTexture
        textureWithContentsOfFile:filename]];
  } else {
    return (SPTexture *) [self registerAsset:filename
      withContent:nil];
  }
}
```

4. Switch to the `Game.m` file, and replace the `AssetsDictionary.h` import with the `TextureManager.h` file in the `import` section.

5. In the `init` method, replace the `AssetsDictionary` test we did earlier in the chapter with the following lines:

```
TextureManager* textureAssets = [[TextureManager alloc] init];
textureAssets.verbose = YES;
[textureAssets registerTexture:@"Default.png"];
[textureAssets registerTexture:@"Default.png"];
```

6. Run the example, and you will get the following output:

```
PirateGame[4925:907] Asset Default.png does not exist. Registering.
PirateGame[4925:907] Asset Default.png already exists. Using cached value.
```

What just happened?

In the first step, we created a `TextureManager` class, which is a subclass of `AssetsDictionary`. In step 2, we defined the `registerTexture` instance method, which we implemented in the next step. A lot happened in this one line, explained as follows:

1. We created an instance of `SPTexture` with the contents of the filename.
2. We registered this instance to utilize `registerAsset` we implemented earlier.
3. We returned the result of the called method.
4. Since the result is of the type `id`, we cast it to `SPTexture`— the type we want.

Now, we go ahead and switch to the `Game.m` file. We replace the line `#import "AssetsDictionary.h"` with `#import "TextureManager.h"`.

Then, we delete the example where we tested out the `registerAsset` method from `AssetsDictionary`. After this, we set up the same test; however, this time we use the `TextureManager` class and the `registerTexture` method. We load the `Default.png` file, which is in the `Resources` folder and is currently just a black image. The `Default.png` file is part of the original Sparrow barebone template.

When we run the example, it loads the image from file the first time, and then it uses the cached result.

Creating a sound manager

Now that we have the texture manager, let's create the sound manager that is going to be very similar to the previous piece of code.

Time for action – implementing a sound manager

To implement the sound manager, just follow these simple steps:

1. Add a new Objective-C class called `SoundManager` derived from `AssetsDictionary` within the **Assets** group.

2. Add an instance method that will register a sound using its filename and return the correct value, as shown in the following code:

   ```
   -(SPSound *) registerSound:(NSString *)filename;
   ```

3. Implement the method from the previous step with the following content:

   ```
   -(SPSound *) registerSound:(NSString *)filename
   {
       if ([_dict objectForKey:filename] == nil) {
       return (SPSound *) [self registerAsset:filename
         withContent:[SPSound soundWithContentsOfFile:filename]];
     } else {
       return (SPSound *) [self registerAsset:filename
         withContent:nil];
     }
   }
   ```

What just happened?

In the first step, we created a `SoundManager` class, which is a subclass of `AssetsDictionary`. In step 2, we defined the `registerSound` method, which we implemented in the next step; this method loads a sound from file and returns the result of the registered asset.

It is very similar to `TextureManager`, but instead of a texture and `SPTexture`, we loaded a sound using `SPSound`.

For now, this is all we will do for sounds and sound management since we don't have any sound assets to load.

Creating a file manager

Now, we almost have a manager for all kinds of assets we want to use. The last thing we need is a manager for our data. We know that data assets can be pretty much anything, so we need to descope the use case for managing data assets. Let's take a look at what we'll need right now:

◆ Loading a plain text file is always a useful piece of functionality. It could contain game texts or a basic level layout.

◆ `NSDictionary` and `NSMutableDictionary` are classes we already used and will be using to store data. How about we load a file and its content is converted to a structure similar to that of `NSDictionary`? The JSON format is very similar to a structure we find in `NSDictionary`, and luckily, since iOS 5, we have the means of converting a JSON file into `NSDictionary` without needing any third-party libraries.

Time for action – managing remaining file types

To create an asset manager for our files, use the following steps:

1. Add a new Objective-C class called `FileManager`, which is derived from `AssetsDictionary` within the **Assets** group.

2. Define an instance method called `registerPlainText`, as shown in the following code:

   ```
   -(NSString *) registerPlainText:(NSString *)filename;
   ```

3. Define another instance method called `registerDictionaryFromJSON`, as shown in the following code:

   ```
   -(NSDictionary *) registerDictionaryFromJSON:(NSString
     *)filename;
   ```

4. Implement the `registerPlainText` method with the following content:

```
if ([_dict valueForKey:filename] == nil) {
  NSString *path = [[NSBundle mainBundle]
    pathForResource:filename];
  NSString *content = [NSString stringWithContentsOfFile:path
    encoding:NSUTF8StringEncoding error:nil];

  return (NSString *) [self registerAsset:filename
    withContent:content];
} else {
  return (NSString *) [self registerAsset:filename
    withContent:nil];
}
```

5. Implement the `registerDictionaryFromJSON` method with the following content:

```
if ([_dict valueForKey:filename] == nil) {
  NSString *path = [[NSBundle mainBundle]
    pathForResource:filename];

  NSData *data = [NSData dataWithContentsOfFile:path];
  NSDictionary *dict = [NSJSONSerialization
    JSONObjectWithData:data options:kNilOptions error:nil];

  return (NSDictionary *) [self registerAsset:filename
    withContent:dict];
} else {
  return (NSDictionary *) [self registerAsset:filename
    withContent:nil];
}
```

6. Add the `example.json` file to the `Resource` folder by right-clicking on the `Resources` folder and selecting **New File....** Select **Other** from the tab and create an empty file. Fill it with the following content:

```
{
    "name": "example",
    "a": 5,
    "b": 6
}
```

7. Now, add `example.txt` to the `Resource` folder, which has the following content:

```
Hello from text file.
```

8. Now that all of our data and the `FileManager` class is set up, let's give it a spin. Switch to `Game.m`, remove the pieces of code that tested our previous asset managers, and import the `FileManager` header file.

9. Add the following piece of code to the initializer method:

```
FileManager* fileAssets = [[FileManager alloc] init];
fileAssets.verbose = YES;
NSDictionary *data = [fileAssets
  registerDictionaryFromJSON:@"example.json"];

NSLog(@"Printing values from dictionary:");
NSLog(@"%@", data[@"name"]);
NSLog(@"%@", data[@"a"]);
NSLog(@"%@", data[@"b"]);

NSLog(@"Loading from text file and displaying as a string:");
NSLog(@"%@", [fileAssets registerPlainText:@"example.txt"]);
NSLog(@"%@", [fileAssets registerPlainText:@"example.txt"]);
```

10. Run the example, and see the following output:

```
PirateGame[5024:907] Asset example.json does not exist. Registering.
PirateGame[5024:907] Printing values from dictionary
PirateGame[5024:907] example
PirateGame[5024:907] 5
PirateGame[5024:907] 6
PirateGame[5024:907] Loading from text file and displaying as a string:
PirateGame[5024:907] Asset example.txt does not exist. Registering.
PirateGame[5024:907] Hello from text file.
PirateGame[5024:907] Asset example.txt already exists. Using cached value.
PirateGame[5024:907] Hello from text file.
```

What just happened?

In the first step, we created a FileManager class, which is a subclass of AssetsDictionary.

In the next two steps, we defined two instance methods: one for loading plain text files and another for loading JSON files.

In step 4, we implemented the registerPlainText method. We could have put it all in a one liner, but that would make it a bit cramped and harder to read. So, if the asset was registered, we returned it using the registerAsset method. We don't need to pass in content this time as the content is already in the dictionary. If it is not registered, we need the path to the filename first. Like every resource we want to load from the **Resource** folder, without the help of third-party libraries, we need to get the exact file location. The [[NSBundle mainBundle] pathForResource] method gives us the exact file location if we pass a filename. The main bundle represents the application bundle of the current app. In the next line, we loaded the file into an NSString, and the encoding is UTF-8. We then returned the result that had been passed through the registerAsset method.

In the next step, we implemented the `registerDictionaryFromJSON` method that works pretty much in the same way as the `registerPlainText` method. However, instead of loading the file into an `NSString`, we used an `NSData` object. We then converted the file contents through the `NSJSONSerialization` class, which offers the `JSONObjectWithData` method. We don't really need to pass in any kind of special options right now.

We added an `example.json` file, which has one key that is a string value and two keys that have number values. In a JSON structure, a key has to be written in double quotes and is a string. A value can either be an array, a string, a number, a Boolean, a null, or an object. If a value is an object, it can have keys and values by itself. So, it can map the structure of `NSDictionary` pretty well.

 For more information on the JSON format, take a look at `http://json.org/`.

In the next step, we added an `example.txt` file and added some content.

In step 8, we removed all pieces of code from the previous example and imported the `FileManager` header file. We set up the file manager like how we did in the previous example. We then called the `registerDictionaryFromJSON` method with `example.json` as its parameter. We already know that we can access values from an `NSDictionary` instance through the `objectForKey` method, but we can also use the square bracket notation, which is more terse and easier to read. Just keep in mind that the square bracket notation for keys requires an `NSString` instance. Values, on the other hand, can be any object or `@` literal such as `@YES`, `@1`, or `@"MyValue"`. Then, we loaded the `example.txt` file and displayed it using `NSLog`.

When we ran the example, we saw when and how the assets were being loaded and the results of the loaded assets.

Our `FileManager.h` file will look like the following:

```
#import "AssetsDictionary.h"

@interface FileManager : AssetsDictionary

- (NSString *) registerPlainText:(NSString *)filename;
- (NSDictionary *) registerDictionaryFromJSON:(NSString *)filename;

@end
```

Our `FileManager.m` file will look like the following:

```objc
#import "FileManager.h"

@implementation FileManager

-(NSString *) registerPlainText:(NSString *)filename
{
    if ([_dict valueForKey:filename] == nil) {

        NSString *path = [[NSBundle mainBundle]
            pathForResource:filename];
        NSString *content = [NSString stringWithContentsOfFile:path
            encoding:NSUTF8StringEncoding error:nil];

        return (NSString *) [self registerAsset:filename
            withContent:content];
    } else {
        return (NSString *) [self registerAsset:filename
            withContent:nil];
    }
}


-(NSDictionary *) registerDictionaryFromJSON:(NSString *)filename
{
    if ([_dict valueForKey:filename] == nil) {
        NSString *path = [[NSBundle mainBundle]
            pathForResource:filename];

        NSData *data = [NSData dataWithContentsOfFile:path];
        NSDictionary *dict = [NSJSONSerialization
            JSONObjectWithData:data options:kNilOptions error:nil];
        return (NSDictionary *) [self registerAsset:filename
            withContent:dict];
    } else {
        return (NSDictionary *) [self registerAsset:filename
            withContent:nil];
    }
}

@end
```

Have a go hero

Our file manager works exactly like we want it to work. There is one little problem if we want to load the same asset as plain text and convert it to NSDictionary from a JSON file. Since we only use a single dictionary for all the file elements, if we load an asset with the registerDictionaryFromJSON method first and later load the same asset with the registerPlainText method, we will get NSDictionary converted into an NSString instead of the text file directly being loaded and added to the dictionary as an NSString.

Basic error handling

For the file manager, we haven't set up any error handling. So, if a file does not exist, the application will probably crash and we will be left guessing why nothing is happening, without any clue how to proceed. For now, we will add some error handling to the registerPlainText method.

Time for action – getting started with basic error handling

To add some basic error handling, take a look at the following steps:

1. Open the FileManager.m file.

2. Update the registerPlainText method to match the following piece of code:

```
-(NSString *) registerPlainText:(NSString *)filename
{
    if ([_dict valueForKey:filename] == nil) {
    NSError *error;

        NSString *path = [[NSBundle mainBundle]
          pathForResource:filename];
        NSString *content = [NSString
          stringWithContentsOfFile:path
            encoding:NSUTF8StringEncoding error:&error];

    if (error != nil) {
      NSLog(@"Error while loading plain text file: %@", error);
    }

        return (NSString *) [self registerAsset:filename
          withContent:content];
    } else {
        return (NSString *) [self registerAsset:filename
          withContent:nil];
    }
}
```

What just happened?

While try-catch blocks are available in Objective-C, it's generally not a good idea to use them as they are quite slow and they can become quite difficult to handle if they are too nested.

The first thing we need is an error object that is a pointer to NSError. When loading the text file, we apply the error handling. If there are any errors when loading the file, the error object is not nil anymore. If this is the case, we log the error.

Have a go hero

This is the most basic error handling at the moment. Here are some suggestions on how to improve it:

- ◆ Catch the case if a JSON file cannot be loaded
- ◆ Catch the case if an invalid JSON file is being processed
- ◆ Add an NSError parameter to register the assets in the file manager

Putting it all together

We now have a couple of different asset managers. It's time to put it all together so that we don't have to instantiate the different managers when we want to use an asset.

Time for action – creating an asset container class

To put all of our asset managers into one single class, use the following steps:

1. Add a new Objective-C class called Assets derived from NSObject within the **Assets** group.

2. Define a static method for each kind of asset, as shown in the following code:
   ```
   +(SPTexture *) texture:(NSString *)filename;
   +(SPSound *) sound:(NSString *)filename;
   +(NSString *) plainText:(NSString *)filename;
   +(NSDictionary *) dictionaryFromJSON:(NSString *)filename;
   ```

3. In the Asset.m file, import all asset managers, as shown in the following code:
   ```
   #import "TextureManager.h"
   #import "SoundManager.h"
   #import "FileManager.h"
   ```

4. For each manager, add a static variable with the appropriate type and set its values to `nil`:

```
static TextureManager *textureAssets = nil;
static SoundManager *soundAssets = nil;
static FileManager *fileAssets = nil;
```

5. We need to overwrite the internal static `initialize` method. Use the following piece of code:

```
+(void) initialize
{
    if (!textureAssets) {
        textureAssets = [[TextureManager alloc] init];
    }

    if (!soundAssets) {
        soundAssets = [[SoundManager alloc] init];
    }

    if (!fileAssets) {
        fileAssets = [[FileManager alloc] init];
    }
}
```

6. Implement each of the static methods by using the correct instance method from each of the asset managers, as shown in the following code:

```
+(SPTexture *) texture:(NSString *)filename
{
    return [textureAssets registerTexture:filename];
}

+(SPSound *) sound:(NSString *)filename
{
    return [soundAssets registerSound:filename];
}

+(NSString *) plainText:(NSString *)filename
{
    return [fileAssets registerPlainText:filename];
}

+(NSDictionary *) dictionaryFromJSON:(NSString *)filename
{
    return [fileAssets registerDictionaryFromJSON:filename];
}
```

7. Switch to the `Game.m` file and update the previous example to use the static `Assets` class:

```
NSDictionary *data = [Assets
  dictionaryFromJSON:@"example.json"];

NSLog(@"Printing values from dictionary:");
NSLog(@"%@", data[@"name"]);
NSLog(@"%@", data[@"a"]);
NSLog(@"%@", data[@"b"]);

NSLog(@"Loading from text file and displaying as a string:");
NSLog(@"%@", [Assets plainText:@"example.txt"]);
NSLog(@"%@", [Assets plainText:@"example.txt"]);
```

8. Run the example. When we check the console, we should see something like what's shown in the following screenshot:

```
PirateGame[5066:907] Printing values from dictionary
PirateGame[5066:907] example
PirateGame[5066:907] 5
PirateGame[5066:907] 6
PirateGame[5066:907] Loading from text file and displaying as a string:
PirateGame[5066:907] Hello from text file.
PirateGame[5066:907] Hello from text file.
```

What just happened?

In the first step, we created an `Assets` class, which is a subclass of `NSObject`.

We defined a static method for each of the asset manager instance methods, such as `texture` for `registerTexture` and `sound` for `registerSound`. Then, we proceeded to the implementation part.

For each asset manager, we defined a static variable: `textureAssets` for our `TextureManager` class, `textureSounds` for our `SoundManager` class, and so on. We set these instances to `nil`.

We had overridden the internal `NSObject` initialize method, which is called once internally and does not need to be called by us.

 More information about how the initialize method of `NSObject` works can be found in the Apple documentation at https://developer.apple.com/library/mac/documentation/cocoa/reference/foundation/classes/NSObject_Class/Reference/Reference.html#//apple_ref/occ/clm/NSObject/initialize.

In the `initialize` method, we allocated and initialized each of the instances if its value was `nil`.

When implementing each of the static methods in the next step, we needed to call the corresponding instance method, such as [textureAssets registerTexture:filename] for the texture method, and we should not forget that we had to return the value of the instance method.

To use the static `Assets` class in our game file, we needed to update the reference to the header file and use the `dictionaryFromJSON` and `plainText` methods from the static class.

When we ran the example, we saw an output similar to the previous example, where we loaded files through the `FileManager`, but in this case we didn't have any message about the assets' statuses as the `verbose` flag was not set to `YES`.

Our `Assets.h` file will look like the following:

```
#import <Foundation/Foundation.h>

@interface Assets : NSObject

+(SPTexture *) texture:(NSString *)filename;
+(SPSound *) sound:(NSString *)filename;
+(NSString *) plainText:(NSString *)filename;
+(NSDictionary *) dictionaryFromJSON:(NSString *)filename;

@end
```

Our `Assets.m` file will look like the following:

```
#import "Assets.h"
#import "TextureManager.h"
#import "SoundManager.h"
#import "FileManager.h"

static TextureManager *textureAssets = nil;
static SoundManager *soundAssets = nil;
static FileManager *fileAssets = nil;

@implementation Assets

+(void) initialize
{
    if (!textureAssets) {
        textureAssets = [[TextureManager alloc] init];
    }
```

```
    if (!soundAssets) {
        soundAssets = [[SoundManager alloc] init];
    }

    if (!fileAssets) {
        fileAssets = [[FileManager alloc] init];
    }
}

+(SPTexture *) texture:(NSString *)filename
{
    return [textureAssets registerTexture:filename];
}

+(SPSound *) sound:(NSString *)filename
{
    return [soundAssets registerSound:filename];
}

+(NSString *) plainText:(NSString *)filename
{
    return [fileAssets registerPlainText:filename];
}

+(NSDictionary *) dictionaryFromJSON:(NSString *)filename
{
    return [fileAssets registerDictionaryFromJSON:filename];
}

@end
```

Before we continue with scene management, let's take a look at how we can use the static `Assets` class when displaying an image.

Time for action – displaying an image

To display an image, we just need to follow these steps:

1. Inside the `Game` initializer method, add the following piece of code:

   ```
   SPImage* image = [SPImage imageWithTexture:[Assets
     texture:@"Default.png"]];
   ```

2. At the bottom of the initializer method, add the image to the display tree of the `Game` class.

3. Run the example, and you will see the following:

What just happened?

As we already know, we need the `SPImage` class to display a texture. It can be compared to `SPQuad`, but instead of just displaying a color, it displays the texture on itself. We used the `Assets` class to get our `Default.png` image from the `Resources` folder.

In the next step, we added the image to the display tree of our game class using the `addChild` method. Running the example we should see that our cardboard puppet doll is not visible anymore because the black image we just loaded is displayed on top of the cardboard puppet doll.

Our `Game.m` file should have the following content:

```
#import "Game.h"
#import "Assets.h"

@implementation Game

- (id)init
{
    if ((self = [super init]))
    {
```

```
        Sparrow.stage.color = 0xffffff;

        SPImage* image = [SPImage imageWithTexture:[Assets
            texture:@"Default.png"]];

    NSDictionary *data = [Assets dictionaryFromJSON:@"example.json"];

    NSLog(@"Printing values from dictionary:");
    NSLog(@"%@", data[@"name"]);
    NSLog(@"%@", data[@"a"]);
    NSLog(@"%@", data[@"b"]);

    NSLog(@"Loading from text file and displaying as a string:");
    NSLog(@"%@", [Assets plainText:@"example.txt"]);
    NSLog(@"%@", [Assets plainText:@"example.txt"]);

        // Our whole cardboard puppet doll code here

        [self addChild:image];
    }
    return self;
}

@end
```

Have a go hero

Now that our asset management system is done, let's discuss a few ways in which we can
improve the setup, which are:

- Right now, if we pass text files into the texture manager, it may load, but it may
  lead to unexpected results once we try to display the texture on the screen. We can
  check for the file extension and only load the asset if it has the correct file extension.

- If we go one step further, we can try to automatically detect which asset we want
  to load by its mime type or, if that's not enough, we can try to detect the file format
  through the magic byte.

- We tested for the functionality of our asset manager, but if we want more thorough
  tests, we may want to resort to unit tests.

What are scenes?

In a typical game, we have a main menu, an options menu, possibly a credits screen, and of course the game itself. We can have all this in a single file, but that will become difficult to maintain after a while. So, it will be a good idea to group these elements into separate entities, which in our case are scenes.

In games that depend on having a lot of levels, such as point'n'click games, it's also a good idea to have scenes for each level.

Time for action – implementing a scene class

To create a scene class, use the following steps:

1. Create a new group called **Scene**.

2. Create a new Objective-C class called Scene, which is derived from the SPSprite class, and save it in the **Scene** group.

3. Add a property called guiLayer, which is a SPSPrite type, as shown in the following code:

   ```
   @property SPSprite* guiLayer;
   ```

4. Add another property called name, which is an NSString, as shown in the following code:

   ```
   @property NSString* name;
   ```

5. Add a third property called director, which is an id, as shown in the following code:

   ```
   @property id director;
   ```

6. Add an initializer that initializes the properties of the class:

   ```
   -(id) init
   {
       if ((self = [super init])) {
           self.guiLayer = [[SPSprite alloc] init];
           self.director = nil;
           self.name = @"scene";
       }

       return self;
   }
   ```

7. Add a second initializer that sets the name of the scene; this should be called `initWithName:`

```
-(id) initWithName:(NSString *) name
{
    self = [self init];
    self.name = name;

    return self;
}
```

What just happened?

Right now, we don't have any scenes, so we can't run the example just yet.

Firstly, we set up the `Scene` class, which needs to be a subclass of `SPSprite` because it needs to be added somewhere and we want to allow all kinds of display objects to be added to the `scene` instance.

We defined three properties; `guiLayer` should be the sprite where all our user interface-relevant display objects will be added, `name` should be the name of the scene itself, and `director` should be the reference to its parent object. In the `init` method, we set default values for these properties. We also added a second initializer, which takes a parameter that sets the name of the scene.

Creating a scene director

Now that we have a basic `scene` class, we need something that can actually manage all the scenes we want to add.

Time for action – managing our scenes with a scene director

To create the scene director, take a look at the following steps:

1. Create a new Objective-C class called `SceneDirector`, which is derived from the `SPSprite` class, and save it in the **Scene** group.

2. Add an instance variable called `_dict`, which is an `NSMutableDictionary` type.

3. Add an instance method that will add a scene to the scene director, as shown in the following code:

```
-(void) addScene:(Scene *)scene;
```

4. Add a second instance method that will add a scene, but this time you are also able to define/overwrite the name of the scene:

```
-(void) addScene:(Scene *)scene withName:(NSString *)name;
```

5. Add an instance method that will show a scene and take NSString as its parameter, as shown in the following code:

```
-(void) showScene:(NSString *)name;
```

6. Let's switch to the implementation. The initializer should initialize the _dict variable.

7. Implement the addScene:(Scene *)scene withName:(NSString *)name method with the following piece of code:

```
-(void) addScene:(Scene *)scene withName:(NSString *)name
{
   scene.name = name;
   _dict[name] = scene;

   scene.director = self;
   [self addChild:scene];
}
```

8. The addScene:(Scene *)scene method should be implemented as shown in the following code:

```
-(void) addScene:(Scene *)scene
{
    [self addScene:scene withName:scene.name];
}
```

9. The showScene method should have the following content:

```
-(void) showScene:(NSString *)name
{
   for (NSString* sceneName in _dict) {
     ((Scene *) _dict[sceneName]).visible = NO;
   }

   if (_dict[name] != nil) {
     ((Scene *) _dict[name]).visible = YES;
   }
}
```

What just happened?

In the first step, we created the class needed for the scene director. This needs to be a
SPSprite because we want an instance of it to be added to the Game class, and the scenes
that the scene director should mange can be added very easily to the scene director.

We defined two instance methods that add a scene: the first method takes the scene, and
the second method takes the scene and a name.

We also needed an instance that actually shows the scene; it takes a name as its parameter.

In the next step, we implemented the initializer of the scene director. We needed to
initialize our NSMutableDictionary. We can do this using the typical alloc-and-init
combination or, alternatively, with the more terse @{} notation.

We implemented the longer addScene method first; we set the scene name to the name
parameter. This overwrites the scene name, even if one has already been given. We then
added the scene to the dictionary, using the square bracket notation which does the same
work as [_dict setObject:scene forKey:name]. In the next line, we set the reference
of the director property within a scene to the current scene director instance. This is
needed; in any other case, we wouldn't have an option to switch from one scene to another
within a scene. We also add the scene to the display tree of the current SceneDirector
instance.

When implementing the shorter addScene, we can just call the longer addScene method
and pass it in the name from the current scene as its second parameter.

The last step is all about showing the scene that has been specified as the parameter. First,
we iterated through all elements in the dictionary, and set its visibility to NO so it won't show
up on the screen; yes, even the scene we want to show. Then, we specifically looked for our
scene in the dictionary and set its visibility to YES.

Have a go hero

Currently, we are loading all our scenes at once. This works for now, but as soon as we have a
lot of scenes, we may be short on memory. To counteract this behavior, we can just have one
scene in the memory at the same time. We may need to have a reference from our
asset to our scene so that we know which asset belongs to which scene.

Pop quiz

Q1. Can a binary data file be considered as an asset?

1. Yes

2. No

Q2. Why should we primarily cache our assets in order to reuse already loaded assets?

1. To reduce CPU cycles

2. To save memory

3. To save disk space

Q3. Can a texture (as in `SPTexture`) be drawn to the screen directly?

1. Yes

2. No

Summary

We learned a lot about asset and scene management in this chapter.

Specifically, we covered how to handle different kinds of assets, cache already loaded files, and implement scenes and mechanisms to manage these scenes.

We also touched on some topics such as textures and displaying an image on the screen.

Now that we know how to handle assets and scenes, we're ready to add the basics of our game—which is the topic of the next chapter.

4

The Basics of Our Game

In the previous chapter, we learned about assets and how to implement our own asset management system which loads the assets from the application bundle and caches them. We used the asset management setup to load our first image. We covered how to group display objects into scenes and wrote a scene director that manages our scenes. In this chapter, we will begin setting up our game. We will learn about what to consider when targeting different devices, and we will take the first step in setting up our game. This includes creating the scenes we need and displaying static images on the screen.

Taking care of cross-device compatibility

When developing an iOS game, we need to know which device to target. Besides the obvious technical differences between all of the iOS devices, there are two factors we need to actively take care of: screen size and texture size limit.

 For a quick reference on the differences between iOS devices, take a look at the comparison table at http://www.iosres.com/.

Let's take a closer look at how to deal with the texture size limit and screen sizes.

Understanding the texture size limit

Every graphics card has a limit for the maximum size texture it can display. If a texture is bigger than the texture size limit, it can't be loaded and will appear black on the screen. A texture size limit has **power-of-two** dimensions and is a square such as 1024 pixels in width and in height or 2048 x 2048 pixels.

When loading a texture, they don't need to have power-of-two dimensions. In fact, the texture does not have to be a square. However, it is a best practice for a texture to have power-of-two dimensions.

This limit holds for big images as well as a bunch of small images packed into a big image. The latter is commonly referred to as a sprite sheet. Take a look at the following sample sprite sheet to see how it's structured:

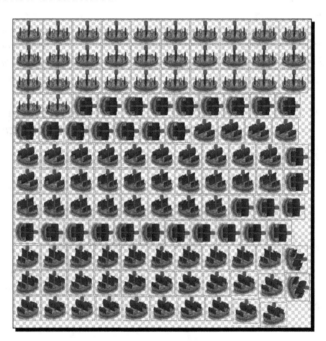

How to deal with different screen sizes

While the screen size is always measured in pixels, the iOS coordinate system is measured in points.

The screen size of an iPhone 3GS is 320 x 480 pixels and also 320 x 480 points. On an iPhone 4, the screen size is 640 x 960 pixels, but is still 320 by 480 points. So, in this case, each point represents four pixels: two in width and two in height. A 100-point wide rectangle will be 200 pixels wide on an iPhone 4 and 100 pixels on an iPhone 3GS.

It works similarly for the devices with large display screens, such as the iPhone 5. Instead of 480 points, it's 568 points.

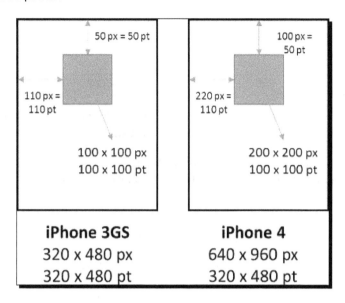

Scaling the viewport

Let's explain the term viewport first: the viewport is the visible portion of the complete screen area.

We need to be clear about which devices we want our game to run on. We take the biggest resolution that we want to support and scale it down to a smaller resolution. This is the easiest option, but it might not lead to the best results; touch areas and the user interface scale down as well. Apple recommends for touch areas to be at least a 40-point square; so, depending on the user interface, some elements might get scaled down so much that they get harder to touch.

Take a look at the following screenshot, where we choose the iPad Retina resolution (2048 x 1536 pixels) as our biggest resolution and scale down all display objects on the screen for the iPad resolution (1024 x 768 pixels):

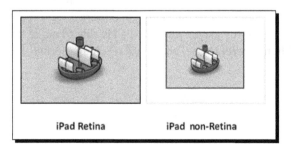

Scaling is a popular option for non-iOS environments, especially for PC and Mac games that support resolutions from 1024 x 600 pixels to full HD.

As we will learn later in this chapter, Sparrow and the iOS SDK provide some mechanisms that will facilitate handling Retina and non-Retina iPad devices without the need to scale the whole viewport.

Black borders

Some games in the past have been designed for a 4:3 resolution display but then made to run on a widescreen device that had more screen space.

So, the option was to either scale a 4:3 resolution to widescreen, which will distort the whole screen, or put some black borders on either side of the screen to maintain the original scale factor.

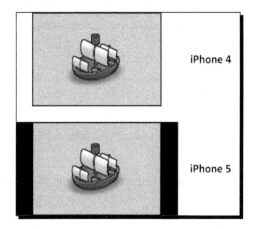

Showing black borders is something that is now considered as bad practice, especially when there are so many games out there which scale quite well across different screen sizes and platforms.

Showing non-interactive screen space

If our pirate game is a multiplayer, we may have a player on an iPad and another on an iPhone 5. So, the player with the iPad has a bigger screen and more screen space to maneuver their ship. The worst case will be if the player with the iPad is able to move their ship outside the visual range for the iPhone player to see, which will result in a serious advantage for the iPad player.

Luckily for us, we don't require competitive multiplayer functionality. Still, we need to keep a consistent screen space for players to move their ship in for game balance purposes. We wouldn't want to tie the difficulty level to the device someone is playing on.

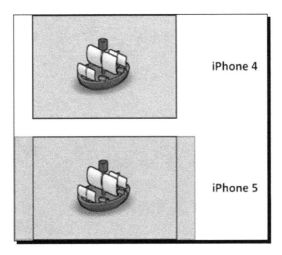

Let's compare the previous screenshot to the black border example. Instead of the ugly black borders, we just show more of the background.

In some cases, it's also possible to move some user interface elements to the areas which are not visible on other devices. However, we will need to consider whether we want to keep the same user experience across devices and whether moving these elements will result in a disadvantage for users who don't have this extra screen space on their devices.

Rearranging screen elements

Rearranging screen elements is probably the most time-intensive and sophisticated way of solving this issue. In this example, we have a big user interface at the top of the screen in the portrait mode. Now, if we were to leave it like this in the landscape mode, the top of the screen will be just the user interface, leaving very little room for the game itself.

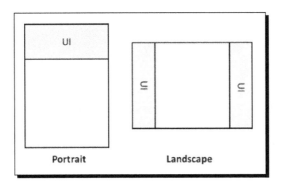

In this case, we have to be deliberate about what kind of elements we need to see on the screen and which elements are using up too much screen estate. **Screen real estate** (or screen estate) is the amount of space available on a display for an application or a game to provide output. We will then have to reposition them, cut them up in to smaller pieces, or both.

The most prominent example of this technique is *Candy Crush* (a popular trending game) by King. While this concept applies particularly to device rotation, this does not mean that it can't be used for universal applications.

Choosing the best option

None of these options are mutually exclusive. For our purposes, we are going to show non-interactive screen space, and if things get complicated, we might also resort to rearranging screen elements depending on our needs.

Differences between various devices

Let's take a look at the differences in the screen size and the texture size limit between the different iOS devices:

Device	Screen size (in pixels)	Texture size limit (in pixels)
iPhone 3GS	480 x 360	2048 x 2048
iPhone 4 (including iPhone 4S) and iPod Touch 4th generation	960 x 640	2048 x 2048
iPhone 5 (including iPhone 5C and iPhone 5S) and iPod Touch 5th generation	1136 x 640	2048 x 2048
iPad 2	1024 x 768	2048 x 2048
iPad (3rd and 4th generations) and iPad Air	2048 x 1536	4096 x 4096
iPad Mini	1024 x 768	4096 x 4096

Utilizing the iOS SDK

Both the iOS SDK and Sparrow can aid us in creating a universal application. Universal application is the term for apps that target more than one device, especially for an app that targets the iPhone and iPad device family.

The iOS SDK provides a handy mechanism for loading files for specific devices. Let's say we are developing an iPhone application and we have an image that's called `my_amazing_image.png`. If we load this image on our devices, it will get loaded—no questions asked. However, if it's not a universal application, we can only scale the application using the regular scale button on iPad and iPhone Retina devices. This button appears on the bottom-right of the screen.

If we want to target iPad, we have two options:

◆ The first option is to load the image as is. The device will scale the image. Depending on the image quality, the scaled image may look bad. In this case, we also need to consider that the device's CPU will do all the scaling work, which might result in some slowdown depending on the app's complexity.

◆ The second option is to add an extra image for iPad devices. This one will use the `~ipad` suffix, for example, `my_amazing_image~ipad.png`. When loading the required image, we will still use the filename `my_amazing_image.png`. The iOS SDK will automatically detect the different sizes of the image supplied and use the correct size for the device.

Beginning with Xcode 5 and iOS 7, it is possible to use asset catalogs. Asset catalogs can contain a variety of images grouped into image sets. Image sets contain all the images for the targeted devices. These asset catalogs don't require files with suffixes any more. These can only be used for splash images and application icons. We can't use asset catalogs for textures we load with Sparrow though.

The following table shows which suffix is needed for which device:

Device	Retina	File suffix
iPhone 3GS	No	None
iPhone 4 (including iPhone 4S) and iPod Touch (4th generation)	Yes	@2x
		@2x~iphone
iPhone 5 (including iPhone 5C and iPhone 5S) and iPod Touch (5th generation)	Yes	-568h@2x
iPad 2	No	~ipad
iPad (3rd and 4th generations) and iPad Air	Yes	@2x~ipad
iPad Mini	No	~ipad

How does this affect the graphics we wish to display? The non-Retina image will be 128 pixels in width and 128 pixels in height. The Retina image, the one with the @2x suffix, will be exactly double the size of the non-Retina image, that is, 256 pixels in width and 256 pixels in height.

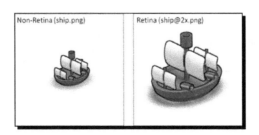

Retina and iPad support in Sparrow

Sparrow supports all the filename suffixes shown in the previous table, and there is a special case for iPad devices, which we will take a closer look at now.

When we take a look at `AppDelegate.m` in our game's source, note the following line:

```
[_viewController startWithRoot:[Game class]
  supportHighResolutions:YES doubleOnPad:YES];
```

The first parameter, `supportHighResolutions`, tells the application to load Retina images (with the `@2x` suffix) if they are available.

The `doubleOnPad` parameter is the interesting one. If this is set to `true`, Sparrow will use the `@2x` images for iPad devices. So, we don't need to create a separate set of images for iPad, but we can use the Retina iPhone images for the iPad application.

In this case, the width and height are 512 and 384 points respectively. If we are targeting iPad Retina devices, Sparrow introduces the `@4x` suffix, which requires larger images and leaves the coordinate system at 512 x 384 points.

App icons and splash images

If we are talking about images of different sizes for the actual game content, app icons and splash images are also required to be in different sizes.

Splash images (also referred to as launch images) are the images that show up while the application loads. The iOS naming scheme applies for these images as well, so for Retina iPhone devices such as iPhone 4, we will name an image as `Default@2x.png`, and for iPhone 5 devices, we will name an image as `Default-568h@2x.png`.

For the correct size of app icons, take a look at the following table:

Device	Retina	App icon size
iPhone 3GS	No	57 x 57 pixels
iPhone 4 (including iPhone 4S) and iPod Touch 4th generation	Yes	120 x 120 pixels
iPhone 5 (including iPhone 5C and iPhone 5S) and iPod Touch 5th generation	Yes	120 x 120 pixels
iPad 2	No	76 x 76 pixels
iPad (3rd and 4th generation) and iPad Air	Yes	152 x 152 pixels
iPad Mini	No	76 x 76 pixels

The bottom line

The more devices we want to support, the more graphics we need, which directly increases the application file size, of course. Adding iPad support to our application is not a simple task, but Sparrow does some groundwork.

One thing we should keep in mind though: if we are only targeting iOS 7.0 and higher, we don't need to include non-Retina iPhone images any more. Using @2x and @4x will be enough in this case, as support for non-Retina devices will soon end.

Starting with the development of our game

Now that we have enough theory and experience with the Sparrow framework, let's put all that knowledge to use and turn theory into practice by creating our pirate game.

> If you miss any of the development of our game, the source code of the game is also available on GitHub at https://github.com/freezedev/ pirategame.

Our game consists of two main gameplay parts:

- **Battlefield/arena**: This is the scene where our pirate ship battles against other ships
- **Pirate cove**: The pirate cove is the hub for activities after battling other ships such as hiring new crew members and upgrading the ship

In this chapter, we will set up the required scenes and load the textures, display them as images, and arrange the entities on the screen.

> The graphics for the game are on GitHub as well: https://github.com/ freezedev/pirategame-assets. The graphics are made with the open-source 3D modeling software, Blender (http://www.blender. org); Version 2.69 is required to open and edit these files. Don't worry, we don't need to update these files for the purposes of this book, but if you want to in order to look for inspiration, you are definitely encouraged to do so.

Let's download the required images for this chapter by navigating to `https://github.com/freezedev/pirategame-assets/releases`. This will show all the available releases for this particular repository, as shown in the following screenshot:

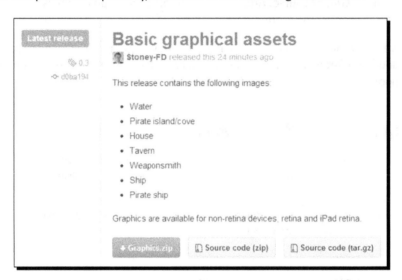

Go ahead and download the `Graphics.zip` package and unzip the contents somewhere on your computer. This package contains the following images:

Filename	Description
`water.png`	This is the background for the battlefield scene.
`island.png`	This is the background for the pirate base. Technically, it's more of an island than a cove, which is why this image is called island, but it's referred to as the pirate cove everywhere else.
`house.png`	This is a shelter for our pirates.
`tavern.png`	This is the building where we get to hire new pirates.
`weaponsmith.png`	This will be the place where we upgrade our ship with additional cannons or ammunition.
`ship.png`	This is our basic enemy.
`ship_pirate.png`	This is the ship we are going to control.

All of the assets are in a non-Retina resolution, Retina for iPad 2, iPad Mini, and iPhone/iPod Touch using the `@2x` filename suffix and `@4x` for iPad Retina devices.

Drag and drop the files into the `Resources` folder of our Xcode project. When a dialog pops up, we need to check **Copy items into destination group's folder (if needed)**, so we don't have to worry about references to the original files. Click on **Finish** to start the process.

So far, the images have been optimized for the landscape mode, so we need to deactivate the portrait mode for now. We need to select the **PirateGame** project and uncheck **Portrait** and **Upside Down** in the **Deployment Info** section, as shown in the following screenshot. Make sure to uncheck them for both iPhone and iPad.

We can also safely delete the cardboard puppet doll code that is still in our Game.m file.

Creating our scene manager setup

In the previous chapter, we created a scene manager which we will now use for our scenes. In our first step, we will need two dummy scenes that we will later fill with gameplay mechanics. We will also need to add these scenes to our scene director and display one of the two scenes.

Time for action – creating our scene manager setup

To create our scene manager setup, we need to follow these steps:

1. Open your Xcode game template if it's not already open.
2. Right-click on the **Classes** folder and select **New Group**.
3. Rename the group to **GameScenes**.
4. Create a new Objective-C class called `PirateCove` which is sub-classed from `Scene`.

5. Add an initializer with the following content:

```
if ((self = [super init])) {
  NSLog(@"Pirate cove scene created");
}
```

6. Create another Objective-C class which is sub-classed from `Scene`. Call this `Battlefield`.

7. Add an initializer with the following content:

```
-(id) init
{
    if ((self = [super init])) {
        NSLog(@"Battlefield scene created");
    }

    return self;
}
```

8. Switch to the `Game.m` file.

9. Add the `PirateCove.h`, `Battlefield.h`, and `SceneDirector.h` files to the `import` section, as shown in the following code:

```
#import "SceneDirector.h"
#import "PirateCove.h"
#import "Battlefield.h"
```

10. In the `init` method, create an instance of the `PirateCove` and `Battlefield` classes and call the `initWithName` method using `@"piratecove"` and `@"battlefield"` respectively for its parameter:

```
PirateCove *pirateCove = [[PirateCove alloc]
    initWithName:@"piratecove"];
Battlefield *battlefield = [[Battlefield alloc]
    initWithName:@"battlefield"];
```

11. Create an instance of the scene director and add it to the `Game` class, as shown in the following code:

```
SceneDirector *director = [[SceneDirector alloc] init];
[self addChild:director];
```

12. Add both scenes to the scene director and show the pirate cove scene:

```
[director addScene:pirateCove];
[director addScene:battlefield];

[director showScene:@"battlefield"];
```

13. Run the example and you will get the following output:

```
PirateGame[4840:907] Pirate cove scene created
PirateGame[4840:907] Battlefield scene created
```

What just happened?

In step 1, we opened our Xcode template from where we left off in the previous chapter. In step 2, we created a new group where everything that is related to our game scenes will be put. In step 3, we renamed the newly created group.

In step 4, we created a new Objective-C class, which is derived from the `Scene` class. In the next step, we added the initializer method where we added a log message to see whether the scene has been created.

In steps 6 and 7, we did the same for the battlefield scene.

After we switched to the `Game.m` file in step 8, we imported all the source files we need, which is the header from the scene director and both scenes we just created.

We created instances of our scenes and our scene director in step 11. The scene director is a sprite itself, so we need to add it to the `Game` class, which also derives from `SPSprite`.

In step 12, we added our scene instances to the scene director, which means that the scenes are now in the display tree. We then called the method in the `SceneDirector` instance to show the battlefield scene.

When we ran the example, we didn't see anything worthwhile on the screen as the scenes didn't have anything in them, but if we take a look at the console, we see that our two scenes have been successfully created.

Here is the full source code from this example:

Pirate cove scene	Battlefield scene
PirateCove.h	Battlefield.h

```objc
#import "Scene.h"

@interface PirateCove : Scene

@end
```

```objc
#import "Scene.h"

@interface Battlefield : Scene

@end
```

PirateCove.m	Battlefield.m

```objc
#import "PirateCove.h"

@implementation PirateCove

-(id) init
{
  if ((self = [super init])) {
    NSLog(@"Pirate cove scene
      created");
  }

    return self;
}

@end
```

```objc
#import "Battlefield.h"

@implementation Battlefield

-(id) init
{
    if ((self = [super init]))
    {
        NSLog(@"Battlefield
          scene created");
    }

    return self;
}

@end
```

The `Game.m` file contains the following code:

```objc
#import "Game.h"
#import "SceneDirector.h"
#import "PirateCove.h"
#import "Battlefield.h"

@implementation Game

- (id)init
{
    if ((self = [super init]))
    {
        Sparrow.stage.color = 0xffffff;
```

```
PirateCove *pirateCove = [[PirateCove alloc]
  initWithName:@"piratecove"];
Battlefield *battlefield = [[Battlefield alloc]
  initWithName:@"battlefield"];

SceneDirector *director = [[SceneDirector alloc] init];
[self addChild:director];

[director addScene:pirateCove];
[director addScene:battlefield];

[director showScene:@"battlefield"];
}
return self;
}

@end
```

Adding images to the battlefield scene

Now that the scenes are ready to use, let's add some ships to the battlefield scene.

Time for action – adding images to the battlefield scene

Let's take a look at the following steps in order to add images to the battlefield scene:

1. Open the `Battlefield.m` file and import the `Assets` header file:

    ```
    #import "Assets.h"
    ```

2. Remove the log message and add the background image, as shown in the following code:

    ```
    SPImage *background = [SPImage imageWithTexture:[Assets
      texture:@"water.png"]];
    background.x = (Sparrow.stage.width - background.width) / 2;
    background.y = (Sparrow.stage.height - background.height) / 2;
    ```

3. Add the pirate ship, as shown in the following code:

    ```
    SPImage *pirateShip = [SPImage imageWithTexture:[Assets
      texture:@"ship_pirate.png"]];
    pirateShip.x = (Sparrow.stage.width - pirateShip.width) / 2;
    pirateShip.y = (Sparrow.stage.height - pirateShip.height) / 2;
    ```

4. Add an enemy ship using the following code:

```
SPImage *ship = [SPImage imageWithTexture:[Assets
  texture:@"ship.png"]];
ship.x = 100;
ship.y = 100;
```

5. Add all children to the display tree, as shown in the following code:

```
[self addChild:background];
[self addChild:pirateShip];
[self addChild:ship];
```

6. Run the example and you will get the following output:

What just happened?

In step 1, we opened the `Battlefield.m` file as this is the file we need if we want to change anything in the battlefield scene and we imported the `Assets.h` file in order to use our asset management system.

In step 2, we prepared the background, which should be in the center of the screen. We used our asset management system to get a texture from a specified file which returns either the cached or newly loaded texture, and the texture will then be used to draw `SPImage` on the screen.

In step 3, we added the pirate ship, which should be in the center of the screen as well. In the next step, we added an enemy ship, which should not be too far away from our ship.

In step 5, we added all our display objects to the display tree, and when we ran the example, we saw two ships on the screen.

The `Battlefield.m` file will contain the following code:

```objc
#import "Battlefield.h"
#import "Assets.h"

@implementation Battlefield

-(id) init
{
    if ((self = [super init])) {
    SPImage *background = [SPImage imageWithTexture:[Assets
      texture:@"water.png"]];
    background.x = (Sparrow.stage.width - background.width) / 2;
    background.y = (Sparrow.stage.height - background.height) / 2;

    SPImage *pirateShip = [SPImage imageWithTexture:[Assets
      texture:@"ship_pirate.png"]];
    pirateShip.x = (Sparrow.stage.width - pirateShip.width) / 2;
    pirateShip.y = (Sparrow.stage.height - pirateShip.height) / 2;

    SPImage *ship = [SPImage imageWithTexture:[Assets
      texture:@"ship.png"]];
    ship.x = 100;
    ship.y = 100;

    [self addChild:background];
    [self addChild:pirateShip];
    [self addChild:ship];
    }

    return self;
}

@end
```

Arranging images in the pirate cove scene

Let's move on to the pirate cove scene to give our pirates a nice little home. What we will be doing in this example is adding a house, a tavern, and a weaponsmith to the scene. These will serve as places where we can update our ship later on.

Time for action – arranging images in the pirate cove scene

To add images to the pirate cove scene, follow these steps:

1. Open `PirateCove.m`.

2. Import the `Assets` header file using the following line of code:

    ```
    #import "Assets.h"
    ```

3. Remove the log message and add the background image, as shown in the following code:

    ```
    SPImage *background = [SPImage imageWithTexture:
    [Assets   texture:@"cove.png"]];
    background.x = (Sparrow.stage.width - background.width) / 2;
    background.y = (Sparrow.stage.height - background.height) / 2;
    ```

4. Add our pirate ship, as shown in the following code:

    ```
    SPImage *pirateShip = [SPImage imageWithTexture:
    [Assets   texture:@"ship_pirate.png"]];
    pirateShip.x = Sparrow.stage.width - pirateShip.width - 120;
    pirateShip.y = Sparrow.stage.height - pirateShip.height - 10;
    ```

5. Add a house, as shown in the following code:

    ```
    SPImage *house = [SPImage imageWithTexture:
    [Assets   texture:@"house.png"]];
    house.x = 100;
    house.y = 100;
    ```

6. Add a tavern, as shown in the following code:

    ```
    SPImage *tavern = [SPImage imageWithTexture:
    [Assets   texture:@"tavern.png"]];
    tavern.x = 220;
    tavern.y = 40;
    ```

7. Add a weaponsmith, as shown in the following code:

    ```
    SPImage *weaponsmith = [SPImage imageWithTexture:
    [Assets   texture:@"weaponsmith.png"]];
    weaponsmith.x = 350;
    weaponsmith.y = 130;
    ```

8. Register all images to the display tree:

    ```
    [self addChild:background];
    [self addChild:pirateShip];
    [self addChild:house];
    [self addChild:tavern];
    [self addChild:weaponsmith];
    ```

9. Go to the `Game.m` file and change the default scene to the pirate cove, as shown in the following code:

```
[director showScene:@"piratecove"];
```

10. Run the example and you will get the following output:

What just happened?

Most of the steps are quite similar to the battlefield scene, so we don't need to explain every step in detail.

In step 1, we opened the `PirateCove.m` file where everything with regard to the pirate cove should be. We needed the asset management system here as well, so we imported it in step 2.

In step 3, we loaded the fitting image, which should be in the center of the screen. In steps 4 to 7, we loaded different entities we wanted to display on the screen, such as the pirate ship and the house. We positioned them more or less randomly on the screen, but left enough space between them so that it won't leave a cluttered impression.

In step 8, we added all of our display objects to the screen. Remember that the order matters. If we were to add the background image last, we will only see the background and nothing else.

We set the scene director to load the pirate cove scene instead of the battlefield scene, and when we ran the example, we saw the pirate cove on the screen.

Pop quiz

Q1. What do we need to actively take care of when developing a universal application?

1. Battery power
2. Screen size and texture size limit
3. GPU memory

Q2. If we want to display an image with the suffix ~ipad, on which device(s) will it load?

1. Non-Retina iPad
2. Retina iPhone
3. Retina iPad

Q3. What will the dimensions be of an image of 256 x 256 pixels on, Retina iPhone in the iOS point coordinate system?

1. 128 x 128 pt
2. 256 x 256 pt
3. 512 x 512 pt

Q4. Which suffix is required to load images on, Retina iPad if the doubleOnPad parameter is set to YES?

1. @2x
2. @3x
3. @4x

Summary

In this chapter, we learned about cross-platform device compatibility between iPad and iPhone devices.

Specifically, we covered which filename suffix we need to identify, which file to load for which device, how the coordinate system in points works, and texture size limits when loading images.

We also set up the bare bone, of our game where we loaded the images for different kinds of devices utilizing our asset and scene managers.

Now that the scenes of our game are available and we have put some images on the screen, we're ready to beautify our game—which is the topic of the next chapter.

5
Beautifying Our Game

In the previous chapter, we learned about cross-device compatibility and what we need to do if we want to target iPhones and iPads simultaneously. We then set up the base for our game. In this chapter, we will begin to add animations to our game.

Working with tweens

Let's say we want to move our ship to an edge of the screen. How would we go about achieving this? The following are two options to achieve this:

◆ Move the ship each frame in the direction we want it to move

◆ Define two states for our ship and let the processor calculate all the required steps for animation

At first glance, the second option seems to be more attractive. We first need to know the initial position of the ship and the position where the ship should be after the animation is complete. Sparrow provides the SPTween class, which does exactly this.

We take two values, also called key frames, and interpolate all values in between. The name "tween" comes from its in-between states.

While in this example, we are talking about moving a position explicitly, in general, a tween is not confined to animating the position of an entity, but could be used to animate its color or any of its other properties.

In Sparrow, specifically, any numeric property of an object can be animated. So every property that is available on an `SPDisplayObject` is available for the `SPTween` class and its animation abilities.

If we want to implement a fade-out or fade-in effect, all we need to do is to animate the `alpha` property of a display object from its maximum to its minimum value or vice versa.

Let's try this by actually moving the pirate ship.

Time for action – moving the pirate ship

Let's follow these steps to move the ship:

1. Open our game project file if it's not already open.

2. Add an instance variable called `_pirateShip` of the type `SPImage`, as shown in following line of code:

    ```
    SPImage* _pirateShip;
    ```

3. Update the references from `pirateShip` to `_pirateShip` in `Battlefield.m`:

    ```
    _pirateShip = [SPImage imageWithTexture:[Assets
      texture:@"ship_pirate.png"]];
    _pirateShip.x = (Sparrow.stage.width - _pirateShip.width) / 2;
    _pirateShip.y = (Sparrow.stage.height - _pirateShip.height) /
      2;
    ```

4. Add a method called `onBackgroundTouch` in the `Battlefield.m` file, as shown in the following line of code:

    ```
    -(void) onBackgroundTouch: (SPTouchEvent*) event
    ```

5. Within this method, get the touch itself:

    ```
    SPTouch* touch = [[event touchesWithTarget:self
      andPhase:SPTouchPhaseBegan] anyObject];
    ```

6. Complete the `onBackgroundTouch` method with the following piece of code:

    ```
    if (touch) {
      SPTween* tweenX = [SPTween tweenWithTarget:_pirateShip
        time:2.0f];
      SPTween* tweenY = [SPTween tweenWithTarget:_pirateShip
        time:2.0f];



      [tweenX animateProperty:@"x" targetValue:touch.globalX -
        (_pirateShip.width / 2)];
    ```

```
    [tweenY animateProperty:@"y" targetValue:touch.globalY -
      (_pirateShip.height / 2)];

    [Sparrow.juggler addObject:tweenX];
    [Sparrow.juggler addObject:tweenY];
}
```

7. Register the event listener to the background image as shown in the following line of code:

```
[background addEventListener:@selector(onBackgroundTouch:)
  atObject:self forType:SP_EVENT_TYPE_TOUCH];
```

8. Switch to the Game.m file.

9. Update the scene director to show the battlefield scene.

10. Run the example and you will get the following output:

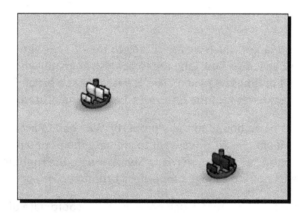

What just happened?

In step 1, we opened our Xcode template from where we left off in the previous chapter. In order to use a pirate ship in the entirety of our battlefield source file, we should move it into an instance variable for the Battlefield class, which is what we did in step 2.

Now, we need to update the references to the pirate ship which was the task for step 3.

After this, we defined the method where we declared what happens if we were to touch the background (in our case, the water on the screen). In step 5, we got the current touch.

In step 6, we implemented the actual tween. As soon as we were sure that we have the current touch object (as in not a false value such as nil), we began to animate the pirate ship.

We created two tweens: the first for the x position of the pirate ship and the second one for its y position. As long as the target and the duration of tween are the same, we could actually use a single tween, as shown in the following code:

```
if (touch) {
   SPTween* tween = [SPTween tweenWithTarget:_pirateShip
      time:2.0f];

   [tween animateProperty:@"x" targetValue:touch.globalX -
      (_pirateShip.width / 2)];
   [tween animateProperty:@"y" targetValue:touch.globalY -
      (_pirateShip.height / 2)];

   [Sparrow.juggler addObject:tween];
}
```

Since we are going to change these properties in a bit, we better leave it at being two separate tweens.

A tween always needs a target which we are setting to the _pirateShip instance variable. Another value we must specify is how long the tween will animate, which is set by the time parameter. The amount of time the tween takes is available as a property on an instance of SPTween. The time parameter is of the type double and is measured in seconds.

The tweenX instance is being bound to the x property. We need to access the property through its NSString identifier. So, if we want to animate the alpha property, we would need to access it through @"alpha". Internally, Sparrow uses the runtime type information (also referred to as reflection) to change properties at runtime.

We set the target value to the current touch position, the x coordinate of that touch to be precise. Now, if we touch the background, the ship's top-left corner would be at the touch position. To feel more natural, we should change it so that the ship is at the center of the touch. This is why we subtracted half of the ship's width from the touch position.

Implicitly, the initial value is automatically set to the current value of the property, which is to be animated.

Then, we did the same for tweenY and the y positions, respectively.

To actually animate the properties, we added the tweens to an object called the juggler, which is available through Sparrow.juggler. We will take a look at how jugglers work later in the chapter.

For the touch event to fire, we registered the onBackgroundTouch method with the background image.

In step 8, we opened the `Game.m` file and updated the `show` call to use the battlefield scene instead of the pirate cove scene that happens in step 9.

Then, we ran the example. If we touch anywhere on the screen, the ship will move to the position we just touched.

Let's take a look at our source files.

The following is the code for the `Battlefield.h` file:

```
#import "Scene.h"

@interface Battlefield : Scene {
    SPImage *_pirateShip;
}

@end
```

Here's the corresponding `Battlefield.m` file:

```
#import "Battlefield.h"
#import "Assets.h"

@implementation Battlefield

-(void) onBackgroundTouch: (SPTouchEvent*) event
{
    SPTouch *touch = [[event touchesWithTarget:self
        andPhase:SPTouchPhaseBegan] anyObject];

  if (touch) {
    SPTween *tweenX = [SPTween tweenWithTarget:_pirateShip
        time:2.0f];
    SPTween *tweenY = [SPTween tweenWithTarget:_pirateShip
        time:2.0f];


    [tweenX animateProperty:@"x" targetValue:touch.globalX -
        (_pirateShip.width / 2)];
    [tweenY animateProperty:@"y" targetValue:touch.globalY -
        (_pirateShip.height / 2)];

    [Sparrow.juggler addObject:tweenX];
    [Sparrow.juggler addObject:tweenY];
  }
}
```

```
-(id) init
{
    if ((self = [super init])) {
        SPImage *background = [SPImage imageWithTexture:[Assets
            texture:@"water.png"]];
        background.x = (Sparrow.stage.width - background.width) / 2;
        background.y = (Sparrow.stage.height - background.height) /
            2;

        _pirateShip = [SPImage imageWithTexture:[Assets
          texture:@"ship_pirate.png"]];
        _pirateShip.x = (Sparrow.stage.width - _pirateShip.width) / 2;
        _pirateShip.y = (Sparrow.stage.height - _pirateShip.height) /
            2;

        SPImage *ship = [SPImage imageWithTexture:[Assets
          texture:@"ship.png"]];
        ship.x = 100;
        ship.y = 100;

        [background addEventListener:@selector(onBackgroundTouch:)
          atObject:self forType:SP_EVENT_TYPE_TOUCH];

        [self addChild:background];
        [self addChild:_pirateShip];
        [self addChild:ship];
    }

    return self;
}

@end
```

Understanding transitions

Let's take a closer look at the animation we just implemented. When we moved our pirate ship, it moves at a constant speed. This is a linear transition, which is the default behavior for each newly created SPTween instance if the transition value is not explicitly set when creating the instance.

The standard way to create a tween with the default transition is as follows:

```
SPTween *myTween = [SPTween tweenWithTarget:_pirateShip time:2.0f];
```

To use a tween with a nonlinear transition, just specify it as a parameter:

```
SPTween *myTween = [SPTween tweenWithTarget:_pirateShip time:2.0f
    transition:SP_TRANSITION_EASE_IN_OUT];
```

In this piece of code, we are using a transition behavior called "ease-in-out", in which case the ship wouldn't move right away but would take its time to start, and shortly before the animation is over, it slows down a bit.

 For a complete list of all available transitions and their graphical representations, take a look at the Sparrow manual at `http://wiki.sparrow-framework.org/_detail/manual/transitions.png?id=manual%3Aanimation`.

Explaining jugglers

The purpose of a **juggler** is to animate other objects. It does this by holding them in a list, and calling an update method every frame. The update method (`advanceTime`) passes through the number of milliseconds that have been passed since the last frame. Every object we want to animate needs to be added to an instance of `SPJuggler`.

The default juggler can be accessed through `Sparrow.juggler` and is the easiest way to animate objects on the screen.

As `Sparrow.juggler` is just an instance of `SPJuggler`, it is also possible to separate jugglers for each of the main components of our game. For now, using the default juggler is enough for our needs.

Updating the movement and canceling tweens

It's time for our first gameplay decisions. Right now, the pirate ship's animation is always 2 seconds long which would provide a serious advantage if the player touched one of the edges of the screen instead of just moving a few points on the screen.

What we need to introduce is some kind of penalty if we move to an edge of the screen, like taking more time for the ship to advance.

It's also a good idea to add the possibility of canceling the animation when the ship is currently moving. So when things get heated, we have a option to retreat from the current battle.

Now, how would we go about implementing the cancelation of the current animation? Let's see the following options for doing so:

♦ By adding a button on the screen

♦ By touching the ship itself

We should try to avoid onscreen controls as long as we can, so let's add this functionality to the touch event (when we touch the pirate ship).

Time for action – updating the movement

To update the movement of our ship, follow these steps:

1. Inside the initializer, add a tween for the enemy ship. We want the enemy ship to move on its own. We should also rename the ship instance to enemyShip:

```
SPImage *enemyShip = [SPImage imageWithTexture:[Assets
    texture:@"ship.png"]];
enemyShip.x = 100;
enemyShip.y = 100;

SPTween *shipTween = [SPTween tweenWithTarget:enemyShip
    time:4.0f transition:SP_TRANSITION_EASE_IN_OUT];
[shipTween animateProperty:@"y" targetValue:250];
shipTween.repeatCount = 5;
shipTween.reverse = YES;
shipTween.delay = 2.0f;

[Sparrow.juggler addObject:shipTween];
```

2. Update the onBackgroundTouch method to resemble the following piece of code:

```
SPTouch *touch = [[event touchesWithTarget:self] anyObject];

if (touch) {
    [Sparrow.juggler removeObjectsWithTarget:_pirateShip];

    float targetX = touch.globalX - (_pirateShip.width / 2);
    float targetY = touch.globalY - (_pirateShip.height / 2);

    float distanceX = fabsf(_pirateShip.x - targetX);
    float distanceY = fabsf(_pirateShip.y - targetY);
```

```
    float penalty = (distanceX + distanceY) / 80.0f;

    float shipInitial = 0.25f + penalty;

    float speedX = shipInitial + (distanceX /
      Sparrow.stage.width) * penalty * penalty;
    float speedY = shipInitial + (distanceY /
      Sparrow.stage.height) * penalty * penalty;

    SPTween *tweenX = [SPTween tweenWithTarget:_pirateShip
      time:speedX];
    SPTween *tweenY = [SPTween tweenWithTarget:_pirateShip
      time:speedY];


    [tweenX animateProperty:@"x" targetValue:targetX];
    [tweenY animateProperty:@"y" targetValue:targetY];

    [Sparrow.juggler addObject:tweenX];
    [Sparrow.juggler addObject:tweenY];
}
```

3. Add a new method called onShipStop as shown in the following line of code:

```
-(void) onShipStop:(SPTouchEvent*) event
```

4. Implement this method with all of the touch boilerplate code and stop all animations:

```
SPTouch *touch = [[event touchesWithTarget:self
  andPhase:SPTouchPhaseBegan] anyObject];

if (touch) {
   [Sparrow.juggler removeObjectsWithTarget:_pirateShip];
}
```

5. Register the onShipStop selector to the pirate ship:

```
[_pirateShip addEventListener:@selector(onShipStop:)
  atObject:self forType:SP_EVENT_TYPE_TOUCH];
```

6. When we add the ships to the battlefield scene, switch the enemy ship with the pirate ship.

7. Run the example and you'll see the following result:

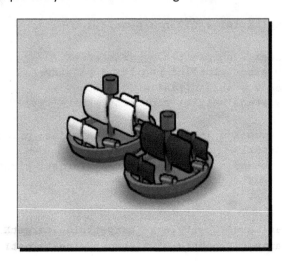

What just happened?

In step 1, we added a tween for the enemy ship right below the code where we load its image.

When creating the instance, we set the time the animation should take to 4 seconds and we used the ease-in-out transition to see the difference when we directly compare it with the default linear transition.

This tween will move the enemy ship by its y property/position. We set the target value to 250, which is more or less the bottom of the screen.

When setting the repeatCount property—which takes an int as its value—we want to repeat the animation for exactly as many times as we set the property to.

Tweens can be reversed by setting the reverse property to YES or NO, as it takes a BOOL value. If we had not set the reverse property in this example, the tween would start at its initial value when repeating the animation. When set to YES, the animation alternates between its initial and target values. We should keep in mind that a reverse animation counts as an animation cycle.

Tweens can be delayed by using their delay property. This property needs a double type as well and is measured in seconds just like the time property.

Now, we need to add the animation to the default juggler.

In step 2, we updated the touch event and the animation. First of all, we removed the andPhase parameter. Previously, we could only move the ship by tapping on the screen. Now, we can either tap the screen or touch-and-drag on the screen to move the ship around.

After we know that a touch was made, we removed all the previously bound tweens from the juggler. Here, we are just making sure that we always have a fresh tween and the pirate ship animation might produce any random side effects such as multiple tweens setting different target values at the same time.

In the next line, we declared and assigned variables for the new position our ship should move to. Then, we got the absolute values between the ship's position and the position of our touch.

The penalty is calculated by the sum of the distances divided by 80, which is conveniently the size of our ship in points. So, the closer the touch is to the ship, the lower this value is, and the further away the touch is from the ship, the higher this value will be.

The speed of the ship, that is, the duration of the animation, is calculated by the relative distance with regard to the screen size multiplied by the square penalty. We also have an initial value of 250 milliseconds, which is the shortest amount the animation could be.

Instead of the `animateProperty` method, we can also use the shorthand method `moveToX:y:` which does the same as calling `animateProperty` on the x and y properties.

In step 3, we added the `onShipStop` method to the source file, which we implemented in the next step. We also removed all tweens with the `_pirateShip` target. So, if currently a tween is being executed, it will be removed.

In step 5, we registered the `onShipStop` event to the pirate ship.

Currently, if we were to move over the enemy ship, the enemy ship would be displayed on the top of our ship. For our ship to be displayed on top of the enemy ship, we need to switch the two around when we add them to the display tree.

After this example, our `Battlefield.m` file should look like the following code:

```
#import "Battlefield.h"
#import "Assets.h"

@implementation Battlefield

-(id) init
{
    if ((self = [super init])) {
        SPImage *background = [SPImage imageWithTexture:[Assets
            texture:@"water.png"]];
        background.x = (Sparrow.stage.width - background.width) / 2;
        background.y = (Sparrow.stage.height - background.height) /
            2;
```

```
        _pirateShip = [SPImage imageWithTexture:[Assets
          texture:@"ship_pirate.png"]];
        _pirateShip.x = (Sparrow.stage.width - _pirateShip.width) /
          2;
        _pirateShip.y = (Sparrow.stage.height - _pirateShip.height) /
          2;

        SPImage *enemyShip = [SPImage imageWithTexture:[Assets
          texture:@"ship.png"]];
        enemyShip.x = 100;
        enemyShip.y = 100;

        SPTween *shipTween = [SPTween tweenWithTarget:enemyShip
          time:4.0f transition:SP_TRANSITION_EASE_IN_OUT];
        [shipTween animateProperty:@"y" targetValue:250];
        shipTween.repeatCount = 5;
        shipTween.reverse = YES;
        shipTween.delay = 2.0f;

        [Sparrow.juggler addObject:shipTween];

        [background addEventListener:@selector(onBackgroundTouch:)
          atObject:self forType:SP_EVENT_TYPE_TOUCH];
        [_pirateShip addEventListener:@selector(onShipStop:)
          atObject:self forType:SP_EVENT_TYPE_TOUCH];

        [self addChild:background];
        [self addChild:enemyShip];
        [self addChild:_pirateShip];
    }

    return self;
}

-(void) onBackgroundTouch:(SPTouchEvent*) event
{
    SPTouch *touch = [[event touchesWithTarget:self] anyObject];

    if (touch) {
        [Sparrow.juggler removeObjectsWithTarget:_pirateShip];

        float targetX = touch.globalX - (_pirateShip.width / 2);
        float targetY = touch.globalY - (_pirateShip.height / 2);

        float distanceX = fabsf(_pirateShip.x - targetX);
```

```
            float distanceY = fabsf(_pirateShip.y - targetY);

            float penalty = (distanceX + distanceY) / 80.0f;

            float shipInitial = 0.25f + penalty;

            float speedX = shipInitial + (distanceX /
              Sparrow.stage.width) * penalty * penalty;
            float speedY = shipInitial + (distanceY /
              Sparrow.stage.height) * penalty * penalty;

            SPTween *tweenX = [SPTween tweenWithTarget:_pirateShip
              time:speedX];
            SPTween *tweenY = [SPTween tweenWithTarget:_pirateShip
              time:speedY];


            [tweenX animateProperty:@"x" targetValue:targetX];
            [tweenY animateProperty:@"y" targetValue:targetY];

            [Sparrow.juggler addObject:tweenX];
            [Sparrow.juggler addObject:tweenY];
        }
    }
}

-(void) onShipStop:(SPTouchEvent*) event
{
    SPTouch *touch = [[event touchesWithTarget:self
      andPhase:SPTouchPhaseBegan] anyObject];

    if (touch) {
        [Sparrow.juggler removeObjectsWithTarget:_pirateShip];
    }
}

@end
```

Working with sprite sheets

So far, we loaded every image on its own and displayed them on the screen. Sprite sheets are a way to combine all of these smaller images into one big image. When we load the image, we are able to use the textures in the same way that we are used to.

When using multiple images, something called a "texture switch" happens every time the current active texture is being swapped out by a different one. This operation is quite heavy on performance, so it should be avoided where possible. Sprite sheets allow us to achieve this by using the same image asset for numerous different images, thus avoiding the texture switch and keeping the number of draw calls to a minimum.

Sprite sheets can also be used for sprite animation, in which a series of images is displayed sequentially one frame after another, which creates the illusion of animation to the human eye—just like a flip book.

A texture atlas is a specialization of sprite sheets with regard to containing smaller images, but it also provides a file of metadata which contains the information of where exactly its subimages are. In practice though, "texture atlas" and "sprite sheet" are used as synonyms.

 Before we get started, let's download all the necessary graphics for this chapter at https://github.com/freezedev/pirategame-assets/releases/download/0.5/Graphics_05.zip.

Learning about texture formats

So far, we only used PNG images. However, let's see if there are any other texture formats in iOS that would better fit our purpose. Spoiler: there are. Leaving the brash remark aside, we are going to analyze which texture formats fits our purpose best.

The following table shows the pirate ship image in different file formats. Let's compare its file sizes:

Compression	File format	File size
None	BMP	257 KB
Lossless	PNG	36.6 KB
Depends	PVR	257 KB
	(In this case RGBA8888)	

When we load a PNG file, what happens internally? The image gets decompressed when it's being loaded—at the expense of the CPU. The same goes for other conventional image formats such as JPEG. Once the image is decompressed, it becomes a texture.

PVR is a texture format specifically optimized for iOS devices or for PowerVR GPUs used on all iOS devices, to be more precise. When loading a PVR image, for example, it will decode the image directly on the GPU instead of the CPU.

PVR includes a lot of different image formats. If we are going for lossless quality including alpha channels, we should opt for the RGBA8888 format. If we don't need the alpha channel, we should use an image format without one. The RGBA8888 image format is not compressed. So, in order to keep the application size at a minimum, we should use the `pvr.gz` format, which is a PVR file compressed using GZIP.

Using TexturePacker to create sprite sheets

TexturePacker is a commercial application to create sprite sheets and texture atlases and is available at `http://www.codeandweb.com/texturepacker` for around 30 dollars. To be able to create our very own sprite sheets, we either need the pro or the trial version of TexturePacker. The TexturePacker download window looks as follows:

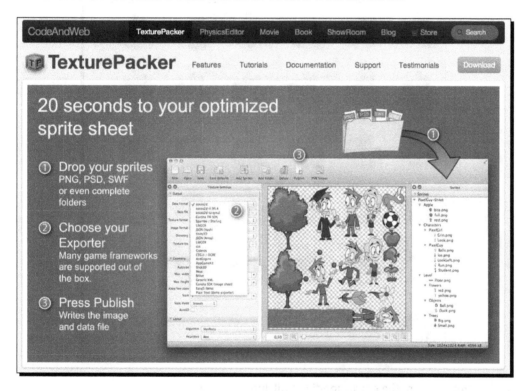

While the workflow is pretty self-explanatory, let's go through a few steps to create our own texture atlas:

1. Drag-and-drop the images `0001.png` to `0032.png` into the **Sprites** section of the application.

2. Select **Sparrow/Starling** as the **Data Format**.

3. Select **GZIP compr. PVR** as the **Texture Format**.

4. Select **RGBA8888** as the **Image Format**.

5. Hit the **AutoSD** button and select **corona @4x/@2x** from the presets.

6. Set the filenames to `ship_pirate_small_cannon{v}.xml` for the data file and `ship_pirate_small_cannon{v}.pvr.gz` for the texture file.

7. Click on the **Publish** button.

Now our texture atlas is generated for each of our resolution we are supporting. Let's take a look at the result. The output of one of the generated images would look like the following screenshot:

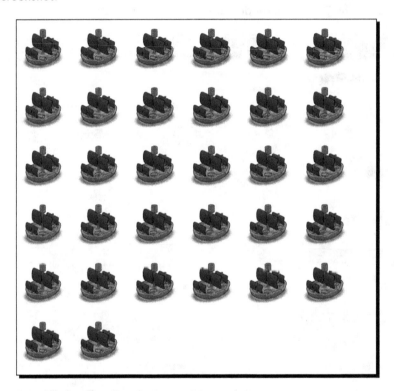

Here's a snippet from the corresponding XML file:

```
<?xml version="1.0" encoding="UTF-8"?>
<!-- Created with TexturePacker http://www.codeandweb.com/
texturepacker-->
<!-- $TexturePacker:SmartUpdate:c58f88c054e0e917cc6c06d11cc04c15:0af47
aa74ca5e538fac63da189c2b7ac:9e0a4549107632fbd952ab702bfc21e4$ -->
<TextureAtlas imagePath="ship_pirate_small_cannon.pvr.gz">
    <SubTexture name="e_0001" x="0" y="0" width="80" height="80"/>
```

```
<SubTexture name="e_0003" x="80" y="0" width="80" height="80"/>
<SubTexture name="e_0005" x="160" y="0" width="80" height="80"/>
<SubTexture name="e_0007" x="240" y="0" width="80" height="80"/>
```

From this snippet, we can see the reference to the original image and its subtextures. Each subtexture has a name, its location inside the bigger image, and its dimensions.

Loading our first texture atlas

Now that we have our texture atlas, let's load and display it with Sparrow.

Time for action – loading our first texture atlas

To load our first texture atlas, we need to follow these steps:

1. Copy the necessary files (`ship_pirate_small_cannon*`) into the project.

2. Load the texture atlas with the following line of code:

   ```
   SPTextureAtlas* atlas = [SPTextureAtlas
     atlasWithContentsOfFile:@"ship_pirate_small_cannon.xml"];
   ```

3. Create an array out of all textures starting with `00`:

   ```
   NSArray* textures = [atlas texturesStartingWith:@"00"];
   ```

4. Create a movie clip object and position it just above the original pirate ship, as shown in the following code:

   ```
   SPMovieClip *cannonShip = [SPMovieClip movieWithFrames:textures
     fps:20.0f];
   cannonShip.x = 200;
   cannonShip.y = 50;
   ```

5. Play the animation with the following piece of code:

   ```
   [cannonShip play];
   [Sparrow.juggler addObject:cannonShip];
   ```

6. Add the animated pirate ship to the display tree as follows:

   ```
   [self addChild:background];
   [self addChild:enemyShip];
   [self addChild:_pirateShip];
   [self addChild:cannonShip];
   ```

7. Run the example to see the following result:

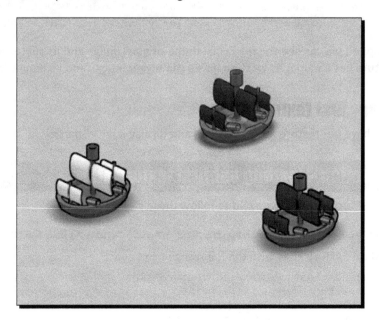

What just happened?

To use the texture atlas, we first copied all related files into the project. Using the `SPTextureAtlas` class, we then loaded the XML file.

In step 3, we needed to get an array (or an `NSArray` to be exact) out of the texture atlas with all of the images starting with `00`, which in our case means that every image in this sprite sheet will be used for the animation.

An `SPMovieClip` class is derived from `SPDisplayObject` and can be added to the display tree as well. It can play the animation from the array we made in step 3. The `fps` parameter is necessary as it sets the speed of the animation.

To play the animation itself, two things need to be done: first, we need to call the `play` method from the movie clip and second, we need to add the movie clip to the juggler. This is exactly what we did in step 5.

In the next step, we added the movie clip to the display tree and when we ran the example, we had our pirate ship, the enemy ship which moves up and down and now the second pirate ship which has the cannon firing animation.

If you want to take a look at the complete source file for this example, it is available at `https://github.com/freezedev/pirategame/blob/71f42ded614c4917802dcba4 6a190476ff7b88c4/Classes/Battlefield.m`.

Pop quiz

Q1. What are tweens?

1.   A way to define animation by setting two key frames

2.   Animations consisting of multiple sprites

3.   A way to optimize multiple display objects on the screen

Q2. What are sprite sheets?

1.   Sketches on a sheet of paper

2.   An image containing several smaller ones

3.   A Sparrow extension to use sprites

Q3. Transitions are used to modify the rate of animation over time.

1.   True

2.   False

Summary

In this chapter, we learned about tweens and sprite sheets.

Specifically, we covered how to animate display objects with tweens, create our own sprite sheets, and how to animate these sprite sheets.

We also touched upon texture formats, jugglers, and transitions.

Now that we have animations and our ship is moving around, let's add some game logic—which is the topic of the next chapter.

6
Adding Game Logic

In the previous chapter, we learned about animating our objects on the screen using tweens; we also learned about sprite sheets, generated our very own sprite sheet with texture information, and animated it.

Let's take a quick look at what kind of topics we will tackle in this chapter:

◆   Shooting cannonballs, which is pretty much a core mechanic of our game

◆   Once a cannonball is displayed on the battlefield, it should be able to collide with the enemy ship

◆   Destroying the enemy ship, if enough cannonballs hit the ship

Extending the asset manager

In the previous chapter, we loaded our very first texture atlas and displayed each subtexture as frames in a movie clip. We did not use our asset manager for this as we hadn't implemented this functionality yet.

So, let's go ahead and allow our asset manager to deal with texture atlases.

Time for action – adding texture atlases to the asset manager

We can extend our asset manager with the following steps:

1. Open our game's project file, if it's not already open.

2. Switch to the `TextureManager.h` file and declare the method `registerTextureAtlas`, as shown in the following code:

```
-(SPTextureAtlas *) registerTextureAtlas:(NSString *) filename;
```

3. Switch to the `TextureManager.m` file and implement the `registerTextureAtlas` method, as shown in the following code:

```
-(SPTextureAtlas *) registerTextureAtlas:(NSString *) filename
{
    if ([_dict objectForKey:filename] == nil) {
    return (SPTextureAtlas *) [self registerAsset:filename
      withContent:[SPTextureAtlas
        atlasWithContentsOfFile:filename]];
    } else {
    return (SPTextureAtlas *) [self registerAsset:filename
      withContent:nil];
    }
}
```

4. Head over to the `Assets.h` file and add the static method `textureAtlas`:

```
+(SPTextureAtlas *) textureAtlas:(NSString*)filename;
```

5. In the `Assets.m` file, implement the following method by referring to its `TextureManager` instance:

```
+(SPTextureAtlas *) textureAtlas:(NSString*)filename
{
    return [textureAssets registerTextureAtlas:filename];
}
```

6. In the battlefield scene (`Battlefield.m`), navigate to where we are loading the texture atlas and getting the textures:

```
SPTextureAtlas *atlas = [SPTextureAtlas
atlasWithContentsOfFile:@"ship_pirate_small_cannon.xml"];

NSArray *textures = [atlas texturesStartingWith:@"00"];
```

Replace the preceding code with the following line of code:

```
NSArray *textures = [[Assets
  textureAtlas:@"ship_pirate_small_cannon.xml"]
    texturesStartingWith:@"00"];
```

7. Run the example. We will see the following constellation of ships on the screen:

What just happened?

In step 1, we opened our Xcode template from where we left off in the previous chapter. In order to load texture atlases, we needed to switch to the texture manager, which we designated to load everything that is remotely connected to textures. In step 2, we declared the method we used in order to use texture atlases through the asset management system. To keep the method names consistent, we will name this method `registerTextureAtlas` to make it similar to `registerTexture`. The signature resembles that of `registerTexture`, but it returns an instance of `SPTextureAtlas` instead of `SPTexture`.

In the next step, we implemented the `registerTextureAtlas` method that loads the texture through the `filename` parameter, and we used the `SPTextureAtlas` factory method just like we did when we learned about texture atlases.

Once we finished extending the texture manager part, we needed to extend the `Assets` class, which we did in step 4 by adding the function head which we implemented in step 5. To keep the naming scheme consistent, we named this method `textureAtlas`. In this method, we just called the `registerTextureAtlas` method of our texture manager and returned the result.

We updated the lines in the battlefield to load the texture atlas for the movie clip through the asset management system. Instead of two lines—one for setting up the texture atlas instance and another for getting the needed textures out of the atlas—we now have only a single line that gets our texture atlas with the `textureAtlas` method from the last two steps and then gets the necessary textures for the movie clip.

When we ran the example in the last step, we had the exact result as we did at the end of the previous chapter, which is a good sign and an indication that the changes work as they should.

Structuring our ships

So far, our ships are just instances of SPImage with tweens attached to them right inside our battlefield scene. In order to keep code duplication to a minimum, let's refactor the ship logic into its own class.

Time for action – creating a ship class

To structure the code of our ship, follow these steps:

1. Add a new group called Entities.

2. Inside this group, add a new Objective-C class called Ship, which is derived from SPSprite.

3. Open the Ship.h file. Add one instance variable for the ship image and another for the movie clip of the ship shooting cannonballs, as shown in the following code:

```
SPMovieClip *_shootingClip;
SPImage *_idleImage;
```

4. Declare an alternative initializer called initWithContentsOfFile, which takes an NSString as its parameter:

```
- (id) initWithContentsOfFile: (NSString *) filename;
```

5. Declare a method called shoot, as shown in the following code:

```
- (void) shoot;
```

6. Declare another method called moveTo that takes the x value as its first parameter and the y value as its second parameter, as shown in the following code:

```
- (void) moveToX: (float) x andY: (float) y;
```

7. Declare a method called stop, as shown in the following code:

```
- (void) stop;
```

8. Define the default initializer for the Ship class with the following lines of code:

```
- (id) init
{
  if ((self = [super init])) {
    NSArray *textures = [[Assets
      textureAtlas:@"ship_pirate_small_cannon.xml"]
        texturesStartingWith:@"00"];

    _shootingClip = [SPMovieClip movieWithFrames:textures
      fps:20.0f];
```

```
    if (_idleImage == nil) {
      _idleImage = [[SPImage alloc] init];
    }

    [self addChild:_shootingClip];
    [self addChild:_idleImage];
  }

  return self;
}
```

9. Now, define the alternate initializer that takes `filename` as its parameter, as shown in the following code:

```
-(id) initWithContentsOfFile:(NSString *)filename
{
  _idleImage = [[SPImage alloc] initWithTexture:[Assets
    texture:filename]];

  return [self init];
}
```

10. Implement the `shoot` method with the following lines:

```
-(void) shoot
{
  [_shootingClip play];
  [Sparrow.juggler addObject:_shootingClip];
}
```

11. The content of the `moveTo` method should look like the following code:

```
-(void) moveToX:(float)x andY:(float)y
{
  [self stop];

  float targetX = x - (self.width / 2);
  float targetY = y - (self.height / 2);

  float distanceX = fabsf(self.x - targetX);
  float distanceY = fabsf(self.y - targetY);

  float penalty = (distanceX + distanceY) / 80.0f;

  float shipInitial = 0.25f + penalty;

  float speedX = shipInitial + (distanceX /
```

```
          Sparrow.stage.width) * penalty * penalty;
      float speedY = shipInitial + (distanceY /
          Sparrow.stage.height) * penalty * penalty;


      SPTween *tweenX = [SPTween tweenWithTarget:self time:speedX];
      SPTween *tweenY = [SPTween tweenWithTarget:self time:speedY];


      [tweenX animateProperty:@"x" targetValue:targetX];
      [tweenY animateProperty:@"y" targetValue:targetY];

      [Sparrow.juggler addObject:tweenX];
      [Sparrow.juggler addObject:tweenY];
  }
```

12. Implement the `stop` method, as shown in the following code:

```
-(void) stop
{
    [Sparrow.juggler removeObjectsWithTarget:self];
}
```

13. Switch to the `Battlefield.h` file and update the class so that the instance variable `_pirateShip` is from the type `Ship`, as shown in the following code:

```
#import "Scene.h"
#import "Ship.h"

@interface Battlefield : Scene {
    Ship *_pirateShip;
}
```

14. Now, switch to the `Battlefield.m` file.

15. Update the `onBackgroundTouch` method in the scene, as shown in the following code:

```
SPTouch *touch = [[event touchesWithTarget:self] anyObject];

if (touch) {
    [_pirateShip moveToX:touch.globalX andY:touch.globalY];
}
```

16. Next, update the `onShipStop` method, as shown in the following code:

```
SPTouch *touch = [[event touchesWithTarget:self
    andPhase:SPTouchPhaseBegan] anyObject];

if (touch) {
    [_pirateShip stop];
}
```

17. Update the remaining references from SPImage to the Ship class and remove all occurrences of the cannon ship, as shown in the following code:

```
_pirateShip = [[Ship alloc]
  initWithContentsOfFile:@"ship_pirate.png"];
_pirateShip.x = (Sparrow.stage.width - _pirateShip.width) / 2;
_pirateShip.y = (Sparrow.stage.height - _pirateShip.height) /
  2;

Ship *ship = [[Ship alloc] initWithContentsOfFile:@"ship.png"];
ship.x = 100;
ship.y = 100;
```

18. Run the example. We now see the pirate and enemy ships on the screen:

What just happened?

In game development, the term entity usually refers to an object on the screen which interacts with other objects. Let's take a 2D action side-scroller as an example: the enemy ships as well as the ship controlled by the player were entities. The bullets were entities too. A bullet, for example, interacted with the player ship as it spawned from it. The enemy ships interacted with the bullets; if a bullet hit an enemy ship, it needed to react by losing hit points or by being destroyed. The same applied to the player ship.

Entities also feature in more advanced game development techniques such as the entity-component pattern, where the interaction is described as components. These components are then attached to entities.

What we need to take away from our game is a clear separation between the different elements of the game. In step 1, we added a new group called Entities. In the next step, we defined our very first entity called Ship, which is a subclass of SPSprite. It was also possible to add a prefix before the class name, just like all Sparrow classes have the prefix SP. For our game, the prefix PG would make sense as it stands for PirateGame.

The ship had two instance variables, which we declared in step 3: one was the cannonball-shooting animation we previously saw in the battlefield scene and the second was the image of the ship itself.

In addition to the default initializer, we declared a second initializer in step 4. This method takes `filename` as a parameter. We didn't want to create a separate class for the pirate ship. We can use the same class for both types. We just needed a different `filename` parameter for either the enemy or the pirate ship.

Our ship class needed to have the following behaviors:

- Shooting (step 5)
- Moving the ship to a certain position (step 6)
- Stopping the movement (step 7)

Our `Ship.h` file now looks like the following code:

```
#import "SPSprite.h"

@interface Ship : SPSprite {
    SPMovieClip *_shootingClip;
    SPImage *_idleImage;
}

- (id) initWithContentsOfFile: (NSString *) filename;

- (void) shoot;

- (void) moveToX: (float) x andY: (float) y;
- (void) stop;

@end
```

Once all methods and instance variables for the `Ship` class were declared, we went on to implement the methods. Before we did that, we defined the initializer in step 8: we initialized the movie clip—with the texture atlas from the shooting pirate ship—and the ship image itself. The only difference to what we know so far is that we are initializing the image if it hasn't been initialized yet.

In the second initializer that we implemented in step 9, we initialized the image with the filename we passed in and we called the default initializer. So, if the alternate initializer was called, we didn't overwrite the `_idleImage` instance variable with a fresh instance of `SPImage`.

The full piece of code of `Ship.m` up to this point is as follows:

```objc
#import "Ship.h"

#import "Assets.h"

@implementation Ship

- (id) init
{
    if ((self = [super init])) {
        NSArray *textures = [[Assets
            textureAtlas:@"ship_pirate_small_cannon.xml"]
              texturesStartingWith:@"00"];

        _shootingClip = [SPMovieClip movieWithFrames:textures
            fps:20.0f];

        if (_idleImage == nil) {
            _idleImage = [[SPImage alloc] init];
        }

        [self addChild:_shootingClip];
        [self addChild:_idleImage];
    }

    return self;
}

- (id) initWithContentsOfFile:(NSString *)filename
{
    _idleImage = [[SPImage alloc] initWithTexture:[Assets
        texture:filename]];

    return [self init];
}
```

In the next steps, we implemented methods for the ship's actions:

♦ **Shooting**: Plays the `_shooting` movie clip (step 10).

♦ **Moving**: This is the moving logic of the ship we previously had in the `backgroundTouch` method in the battlefield scene. Instead of removing all tweens from the ship instance, we called the `stop` method from the `ship` instance (step 11).

♦ **Stopping**: Removes all tweens from the current instance (step 12).

In its completeness, these methods look like the following piece of code:

```objc
-(void) shoot
{
    [_shootingClip play];
    [Sparrow.juggler addObject:_shootingClip];
}

-(void) moveToX:(float)x andY:(float)y
{
    [self stop];

    float targetX = x - (self.width / 2);
    float targetY = y - (self.height / 2);

    float distanceX = fabsf(self.x - targetX);
    float distanceY = fabsf(self.y - targetY);

    float penalty = (distanceX + distanceY) / 80.0f;

    float shipInitial = 0.25f + penalty;

    float speedX = shipInitial + (distanceX / Sparrow.stage.width) *
        penalty * penalty;
    float speedY = shipInitial + (distanceY / Sparrow.stage.height) *
        penalty * penalty;

    SPTween *tweenX = [SPTween tweenWithTarget:self time:speedX];
    SPTween *tweenY = [SPTween tweenWithTarget:self time:speedY];


    [tweenX animateProperty:@"x" targetValue:targetX];
    [tweenY animateProperty:@"y" targetValue:targetY];

    [Sparrow.juggler addObject:tweenX];
    [Sparrow.juggler addObject:tweenY];
}

-(void) stop
{
    [Sparrow.juggler removeObjectsWithTarget:self];
}

@end
```

In the last steps, we updated the battlefield scene. First, we updated the header file. We needed to import the `Ship.h` file, and instead of being a pointer to `SPImage`, the `_pirateShip` instance variable was a pointer to the `Ship` class.

After this step, our `Battlefield.h` file had the following content:

```objc
#import "Scene.h"
#import "Ship.h"

@interface Battlefield : Scene {
    Ship* _pirateShip;
}

@end
```

We updated the touch interactions in the battlefield scene:

- onBackgroundTouch: Since we moved the movement logic to the `Ship` class, we just needed to call the correct method, which was `moveTo`, and pass in the *x* and *y* coordinate of `touch` (step 15)

- onShipStop: Similar to the `moveTo` method, we just needed to call the `stop` method of the ship itself (step 16)

The touch events inside the `Battlefield.m` file should resemble the following piece of code:

```objc
#import "Battlefield.h"
#import "Assets.h"

@implementation Battlefield

-(void) onBackgroundTouch:(SPTouchEvent*) event
{
    SPTouch *touch = [[event touchesWithTarget:self] anyObject];

    if (touch) {
        [_pirateShip moveToX:touch.globalX andY:touch.globalY];
    }
}

-(void) onShipStop:(SPTouchEvent*) event
{
    SPTouch *touch = [[event touchesWithTarget:self
      andPhase:SPTouchPhaseBegan] anyObject];
```

```
        if (touch) {
            [_pirateShip stop];
        }
    }
}
```

In the next step, we updated the initializer for the ships. We didn't need the `cannonShip` movie clip anymore as this was an instance variable inside the `Ship` class.

Let's take a look at the initializer in the following code that binds these touch selectors and sets up the ship itself:

```
-(id) init
{
    if ((self = [super init])) {
        SPImage *background = [SPImage imageWithTexture:[Assets
            texture:@"water.png"]];
        background.x = (Sparrow.stage.width - background.width) / 2;
        background.y = (Sparrow.stage.height - background.height) /
            2;

        _pirateShip = [[Ship alloc]
            initWithContentsOfFile:@"ship_pirate.png"];
        _pirateShip.x = (Sparrow.stage.width - _pirateShip.width) /
            2;
        _pirateShip.y = (Sparrow.stage.height - _pirateShip.height) /
            2;


        Chip *ship = [[Ship alloc]
            initWithContentsOfFile:@"ship.png"];
        ship.x = 100;
        ship.y = 100;

        SPTween *shipTween = [SPTween tweenWithTarget:ship time:4.0f
            transition:SP_TRANSITION_EASE_IN_OUT];
        [shipTween animateProperty:@"y" targetValue:250];
        shipTween.repeatCount = 5;
        shipTween.reverse = YES;
        shipTween.delay = 2.0f;

        [Sparrow.juggler addObject:shipTween];
```

```
            [background addEventListener:@selector(onBackgroundTouch:)
              atObject:self forType:SP_EVENT_TYPE_TOUCH];
            [_pirateShip addEventListener:@selector(onShipStop:)
              atObject:self forType:SP_EVENT_TYPE_TOUCH];
            [self addChild:background];
            [self addChild:ship];
            [self addChild:_pirateShip];
        }

        return self;
    }

    @end
```

When we ran the example, we saw two ships on the screen; if we tapped anywhere, our pirate ship moved to that point, just like we expected it to. If we touched the ship during movement, it stopped.

Extending the ship class

Now that the base of our ship class is done, let's think of what we need for the ship class:

- **Hit points**: If a ship is hit, the hit points should reflect this state. The ship will start out with a given number of hit points, say 20 for example, and it will lose some each time it is hit. When it finally reaches zero hit points, it will be completely destroyed.

- **Direction**: This is the direction the ship is facing. Depending on the direction, the cannonballs will be fired from each side of the ship.

We should abstain from using filenames where we don't necessarily need to, for example now, when initializing our ship instances.

Before we go ahead and get to the coding part of things, let's download the latest images from https://github.com/freezedev/pirategame-assets/releases/download/0.6/Graphics_06.zip. These images include updated sprite sheets for both the pirate ship and a cannonball that we will use later.

Delete the ship_small_cannon files and copy the newer files to the project. This can be done easily, but Xcode doesn't always like replacing existing files.

Time for action – adding more functionality to the ship class

Let's extend the ship class using the following steps:

1. Open the `Ship.h` file.

2. Add `enum` for the eight directions of the ship, as shown in the following code:

    ```
    typedef NS_ENUM(NSInteger, ShipDirection) {
        DirectionNorth,
        DirectionSouth,
        DirectionWest,
        DirectionEast,
        DirectionNorthWest,
        DirectionNorthEast,
        DirectionSouthWest,
        DirectionSouthEast
    };
    ```

3. Add another `enum` for the type of the ship, as shown in the following code:

    ```
    typedef NS_ENUM(NSInteger, ShipType) {
        ShipPirate,
        ShipNormal
    };
    ```

4. Change the `_shootingClip` instance variable to be a pointer to the `NSArray` class and remove the `_idleImage` instance variable, as shown in the following code:

    ```
    NSArray *_shootingClip;
    ```

5. Add a property for the ship's `hitpoints`, as shown in the following line of code:

    ```
    @property int hitpoints;
    ```

6. Add another property for `type`, as shown in the following line of code:

    ```
    @property ShipType type;
    ```

7. The third property is the direction of the ship:

    ```
    @property (nonatomic) ShipDirection direction;
    ```

    Because we will need to write custom getters and setters for this property as well, we will need an instance variable of the same name, prefixed with an underscore:

    ```
    @interface Ship : SPSprite {
        NSArray *_shootingClip;
        ShipDirection _direction;
    }
    ```

8. Replace the `initWithContentsOfFile` method declaration with `initWithType`. This method takes `ShipType` as its parameter, as shown in the following line of code:

```
-(id)initWithType:(ShipType)type;
```

9. Switch to the `Ship.m` file.

10. Let's implement the `initWithType` method with the following lines of code:

```
-(id) initWithType:(ShipType)type
{
    if ((self = [super init])) {
        self.hitpoints = 100;
        self.type = type;

        SPTextureAtlas *atlas = (type == ShipPirate) ? [Assets
            textureAtlas:@"ship_pirate_small_cannon.xml"] :
              [Assets textureAtlas:@"ship_small_cannon.xml"] ;

        NSArray *texturesNorth = [atlas
          texturesStartingWith:@"n_00"];
        // ...

        float animationFPS = 12.0f;

        SPMovieClip *clipNorth = [SPMovieClip
          movieWithFrames:texturesNorth fps:animationFPS];
        // ...

        _shootingClip = [NSArray arrayWithObjects:clipNorth,
            clipSouth, clipWest, clipEast, clipNorthWest,
              clipNorthEast, clipSouthWest, clipSouthEast, nil];

        for (SPMovieClip* clip in _shootingClip) {
            clip.loop = NO;
            [self addChild:clip];
        }

        self.direction = DirectionSouthWest;
    }

    return self;
}
```

11. Remove the `initWithContentsOfFile` method and update the default initializer to use the `initWithType` method, as shown in the following code:

```
-(id) init
{
    return [self initWithType:ShipNormal];
}
```

12. Implement the custom getter for the `direction` property by simply returning the `_direction` instance variable.

13. The setter for the `direction` property needs to have the following code:

```
_direction = direction;

for (SPMovieClip* clip in _shootingClip) {
  clip.visible = NO;
}

((SPMovieClip *) _shootingClip[_direction]).visible = YES;
```

14. Replace the content of the `shoot` method with the following lines:

```
for (SPMovieClip* clip in _shootingClip) {
  [Sparrow.juggler removeObjectsWithTarget:clip];
}

[_shootingClip[self.direction] play];
[Sparrow.juggler addObject:_shootingClip[self.direction]];

[_shootingClip[self.direction]
  addEventListenerForType:SP_EVENT_TYPE_COMPLETED
    block:^(SPEvent *event)
{
    [_shootingClip[self.direction] stop];
}];
```

15. Within the `moveTo` method, after the creation of the `tweenX` and `tweenY` objects, declare and define two variables that should detect which direction the ship will be rotated to, as shown in the following code:

```
int signX = 0;
int signY = 0;
```

16. Only update the values if a certain threshold has been broken, as shown in the following code:

```
if (distanceX > 40) {
  signX = (self.x - targetX) / distanceX;
}


if (distanceY > 40) {
  signY = (self.y - targetY) / distanceY;
}
```

17. Change `direction` to `DirectionEast` if `signX` has the value `1` and `signY` still has the value `0`, as shown in the following code:

```
if ((signX == 1) && (signY == 0)) {
  self.direction = DirectionEast;
}
```

18. Repeat this for all the remaining directions.

19. Switch to the `Battlefield.m` file.

20. Update the initializers to the pirate and enemy ships. Only the pirate ship needs to have the `PirateShip` value from the `ShipType` type.

21. Inside the `onShipStop` method, add the functionality to shoot when the pirate ship is tapped twice and stop if the ship is tapped once, as shown in the following code:

```
if (touch) {
  if (touch.tapCount == 1) {
    [_pirateShip stop];
  } else if (touch.tapCount == 2) {
    [_pirateShip shoot];
  }
}
```

22. Rename `onShipStop` and all its references to `onShipTap`.

23. Run the example.

We now see that the ship is moving in the direction where we touched the screen.

What just happened?

First, we opened the ship header file, and then we defined an enum for all the direction states. Objective-C provides a handy NS_ENUM macro which lets us do exactly that. As the first parameter, we need the type the enum will be represented as. The second parameter is the name of the enum type. This enum type has eight states: north, south, west, east, and a combination of these.

In step 3, we defined a second enum for the type of ship. It can either be a pirate ship or a normal enemy ship without black flags.

In step 4, we redefined the type of the _shootingClip instance. The reasoning behind this change is that we hold all movie clips in an array and can access a specific movie clip through the index.

In the next few steps, we added a few properties to the class, as listed:

- hitpoints: This indicates how many hit points the ship currently has (step 5)
- type: This indicates the type of the ship (step 6)
- direction: This indicates the direction the ship is facing (step 7)

While it would have been fine to just add the filename to each initializer call when we created an instance of the ship class, it would get messy once we either changed all of these filenames or if we had more than just a few ships on the screen. This is why we replaced the initWithContentsOfFile method with the initWithType method.

Next, we implemented all of the methods we just declared. We started with the one we declared last. As this was our go-to initializer, we got through what was happening here:

- We set the hitpoints property to 100. While 100 is more or less a random number, it is a good starting point to balance from as it's very easy to calculate with. For example, let's say we require four hits to destroy any ships; the damage potential of a cannonball is 25.

- We set the `type` property to the value of the `type` parameter.

- We set the texture atlas to either the pirate ship atlas or the other option, depending on the type. A ternary operation was just a fancy way of writing an `if` statement, as shown in the following line of code:

```
if (type == ShipPirate) { ... } else { ... }
```

  The advantage of the ternary operation was that we could assign its result directly to a variable.

- We got the textures for each direction. Within the texture atlas, every direction of the shooting animation was prefixed with the abbreviation of the direction: `n` for north, `nw` for northwest, and so on.

- We then defined the speed for the animations. We set it to 12 frames per second as we didn't want the animation to be slower than usual. After all, operating the cannons is tough.

- Just like we made an instance of `NSArray` for every direction, we needed to do the same for all the movie clips. We could also write this line as follows:

```
_shootingClip = @[clipNorth, clipSouth, clipWest, clipEast,
    clipNorthWest, clipNorthEast, clipSouthWest, clipSouthEast];
```

- We added all movie clips to the `_shootingClip` instance variable.

- All the movie clips were added to the display tree by iterating over the `_shootingClip` instance variable. We also wanted the movie clips to play only once, which is why we set the `loop` property to `NO`.

- The default direction of a ship was south-west.

In step 11, we significantly simplified the default initializer by just calling the `initWithType` initializer with the `ShipNormal` type.

We started with creating the custom getters and setters for the `direction` property. We added the `nonatomic` keyword to the property definition. This was a performance optimization method to make the generated accessor faster, but non-thread safe. Since Sparrow should only be used single-threaded, it was safe to use `nonatomic` in our game. Internally, Objective-C had already defined the getters and setters as `propertyName` and `setPropertyName`, or in our case, `direction` and `setDirection`.

To use our own code, we just needed to overwrite these methods. The getter for the `direction` property was pretty simple as it just needed to return the `_direction` instance variable.

In our custom setter for the `direction` property, we needed to set the instance variable `_direction` to the value of the parameter first. Then, we iterated through all the movie clips and set its `visible` property to `NO`. We then showed the movie clip of the current direction. This was very similar to how we show scenes through the scene director.

In step 14, we updated the shoot method using the following steps:

◆ We removed all animatable objects from the juggler which originate from any of the movie clips.

◆ We played the movie clip from the current direction and added it to the juggler.

◆ We added an event listener to the movie clip that fired when the movie clip animation was complete. Instead of a selector, we used a block. A block (also called a closure in non-Objective-C environments) is a function which has access to non-local variables. So, while we could define variables inside the block, we accessed the variables as if we were declaring a statement inside the shoot method. A block had a certain appeal to it as we didn't need to define a separate selector for just a few lines of code. There were few things we needed to be careful about when using blocks, but Xcode usually warned us about potential side effects.

◆ Inside our block, we stopped the movie clip as it didn't reset itself. It was like rewinding a VHS tape.

At this time, we updated the ship's direction when it moved. To achieve this, we defined two variables inside the moveTo method: signX and signY. Their default values were 0.

The idea behind that was to map the direction from the values we got in our moveTo method to a value from the ShipDirection values. If signY was 1, it would map to DirectionNorth; if signX was -1, it would map to DirectionWest; and if both had the values at the same time, they would map to DirectionNorthWest.

We had set the signX variables to the *x* coordinate of the object minus the target *x* coordinate and dividing that by distanceX. So, our values for signX were either 1 or -1. The same happened for the signY variable.

Now, if we moved the ship, we only got directions such as DirectionNorthWest, DirectionNorthEast, DirectionSouthEast, and DirectionSouthWest. It is pretty much impossible to tap the same pixel on a line twice. This was why we needed a threshold. We only set signX and signY to 1 or -1, respectively, if distance was more than 40 points. In this case, 40 was not a random number; a rectangle with 40 x 40 points is the average size of a tap, according to Apple.

In steps 17 and 18, we mapped the signX and signY variables to the ShipDirection values, and we set the direction property accordingly.

Within the battlefield scene, we needed to create our ship instances. For the enemy ship, we used the default initializer.

In step 21, we updated the onShipStop method. We utilized the tapCount property of the touch object to see how many times the object had been tapped. If the ship had been tapped once, it would stop its movement, and if it had been tapped twice, it would shoot.

Since the `onShipStop` method did not only stop the ship but also shot if tapped twice, it was a good call to rename this method to `onShipTap`.

When we ran the example, the ship changed its direction depending on where we tapped on the screen, and when we double-tapped the ship, we saw the cannon animation.

Shooting cannonballs

When we double-tap our ship, the animation plays. However, there is one obvious thing missing, the cannonballs! Let's go ahead and add some cannonballs.

Time for action – allowing the ship to shoot cannonballs

Let's allow the pirate ship to shoot cannonballs by following these steps:

1. Open the `Ship.h` file.

2. Add a read-only property called `isShooting`, which has an instance variable counterpart called `_isShooting`, as shown in the following code:

   ```
   @property (readonly) BOOL isShooting;
   ```

3. Add a cannonball for the left-hand side and the right-hand side of the ship. Both of them are pointers to `SPImage`, as shown in the following code:

   ```
   @property SPImage *cannonBallLeft;
   @property SPImage *cannonBallRight;
   ```

4. Switch to the `Ship.m` file.

5. Inside the `initWithType` method, set the `_isShooting` instance variable to `NO` at the top of the method.

6. Inside the `initWithType` method, create both cannonballs with the `cannonball.png` image, set their `visible` property to `NO`, and add them to the display tree.

7. Inside the `shoot` method, abort if `_isShooting` is set to `YES`, else set `_isShooting` to `YES`, as shown:

   ```
   if (_isShooting) {
     return;
   }

   _isShooting = YES;
   ```

8. Set some default values for the animation speed and target position, as shown in the following code:

```
float shootingTime = 1.25f;
float innerBox = 25.0f;
float targetPos = 30.0f;
```

9. Add a reference to the movie clip with the current direction, as shown in the following line of code:

```
SPMovieClip *currentClip = _shootingClip[self.direction];
```

10. Create a tween object for each cannonball and their respective *x* and *y* properties:

```
SPTween *tweenCbLeftX = [SPTween
    tweenWithTarget:self.cannonBallLeft time:shootingTime];
SPTween *tweenCbLeftY = [SPTween
    tweenWithTarget:self.cannonBallLeft time:shootingTime];
SPTween *tweenCbRightX = [SPTween
    tweenWithTarget:self.cannonBallRight time:shootingTime];
SPTween *tweenCbRightY = [SPTween
    tweenWithTarget:self.cannonBallRight time:shootingTime];
```

11. Set up the cannonballs and their tween properties for a direction pair, as shown in the following code:

```
switch (self.direction) {
  case DirectionNorth:
  case DirectionSouth:
    self.cannonBallLeft.x = (-self.cannonBallLeft.width / 2) +
      innerBox;
    self.cannonBallLeft.y = (currentClip.height -
      self.cannonBallLeft.height) / 2;

    self.cannonBallRight.x = (-self.cannonBallRight.width / 2)
      + currentClip.width - innerBox;
    self.cannonBallRight.y = (currentClip.height -
      self.cannonBallRight.height) / 2;

    [tweenCbLeftX animateProperty:@"x"
      targetValue:self.cannonBallLeft.x - targetPos];
    [tweenCbRightX animateProperty:@"x"
      targetValue:self.cannonBallRight.x + targetPos];

    break;

  default:
    break;
}
```

12. Set up the cannonballs for the `DirectionEast`/`DirectionWest` pair.

13. Set both cannonballs to be visible on the screen and add all cannonball-related tweens to the main juggler.

14. Remove all tweens that originate from the cannonballs just after the line where we removed all tweens originating from the movie clips.

15. Once the movie clip is finished, set the `_isShooting` instance variable to `NO` and hide both cannonballs.

16. Run the example. Our pirate ship can now shoot cannonballs, as shown in the following screenshot:

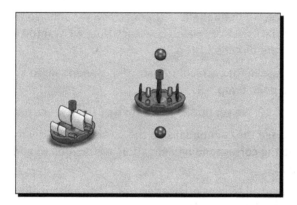

What just happened?

We started this example in the header file of the `Ship` class, where we added a few new properties, such as:

- `isShooting`: This indicates if the ship is currently shooting (step 2)
- `cannonBallLeft`: This indicates the cannonball shooting from the left-hand side of the ship (step 3)
- `cannonBallRight`: This indicates the cannonball shooting from the right-hand side of the ship (step 3)

In the next steps, we modified the `initWithType` method using the following steps:

- We set `_isShooting` to a default value, which is `NO` (step 5)
- We created the cannonball objects (step 6)
- We hid both cannonballs (step 6)
- We added the cannonballs to the display tree (step 6)

Let's head into the shoot method and see what changed here:

◆ We only executed the method if the ship was not shooting to minimize potential side effects and prevent someone from tapping on the ship all the time (step 7).

◆ We defined the variable shootingTime at the time the shooting took place. It is set to 1.2 seconds because this is the approximate length of the movie clip animation (step 8).

◆ The variable innerBox was the distance from the edge of the ship image to the actual image itself (step 8).

◆ The variable targetPos stored how far the cannonballs would fly (step 8).

◆ For convenience, we defined the currentClip variable, so we didn't have to type _shootingClip[self.direction] each time we wanted to access the movie clip of the current direction (step 9).

◆ We defined a tween for each coordinate and cannonball, so in total, we had four tweens at this point (step 10).

◆ In steps 11 and 12, we set up the positions and the tweens for the cannonballs.

◆ We needed to see the cannonballs on the screen, which is why we set them to be visible. To see the corresponding animation, we needed to add the tweens to the juggler (step 13).

◆ We also removed all tweens originating from the cannonballs before we actually played the animation (step 14).

◆ The last thing we needed to update in the shoot method was setting the _isShooting instance variable to NO once the animation was complete, and we hid both cannonballs in the same block (step 15).

When we ran the example and double-tapped our pirate ship, the movie clip played and two huge cannonballs emerged from both sides of the ship.

Have a go hero

So far, the ship cannot shoot diagonally. Go ahead and implement this functionality on your own.

Collision detection

Before we implement collision detection, let's take a look at different types of collision detections:

◆ **Bounding box collision**: We check the bounds of the entities (which is a rectangle). If these rectangles intersect, we have a collision.

◆ **Bounding sphere collision**: We calculate the distance between two entities. If the distance is smaller than the radius of both entities combined, these entities are colliding.

◆ **Pixel collision**: We check if all the pixels of one entity intersect with the pixels of another entity. While this is definitely the most detailed and comprehensive collision check, it is also the most CPU-intensive one.

Now that our pirate ship is actually shooting cannonballs, let's implement the functionality that can hit and sink the enemy ship. We use the bounding box collision because this is one of the easiest collision detection types to implement.

Time for action – letting cannonballs collide with ships

To check if cannonballs collide against the enemy ship, follow these steps:

1. Open the `Ship.h` file.

2. We need to add custom getters and setters to the `hitpoints` property, so let's make this property `nonatomic` and add an instance variable called `_hitpoints`.

3. Declare the methods `abortShooting` and `hit`.

4. Switch to the `Ship.m` file.

5. The custom `hitpoints` getter just returns the instance variable `_hitpoints`.

6. The custom setter for `hitpoints` contains the following code:

```
-(void) setHitpoints:(int)hitpoints
{
    _hitpoints = hitpoints;
    if (_hitpoints <= 0) {
        self.visible = NO;
    }
}
```

7. The `abortShooting` method consists of the following lines:

```
-(void) abortShooting
{
    _isShooting = NO;

    [Sparrow.juggler
      removeObjectsWithTarget:self.cannonBallLeft];
    [Sparrow.juggler
      removeObjectsWithTarget:self.cannonBallRight];

    self.cannonBallLeft.visible = NO;
    self.cannonBallRight.visible = NO;
}
```

8. The `hit` method has the following content:

```
-(void) hit
{
    self.hitpoints = self.hitpoints - 25;

    for (SPMovieClip* clip in _shootingClip) {
        SPTween *tween = [SPTween tweenWithTarget:clip
            time:0.3f];
        tween.reverse = YES;
        tween.repeatCount = 2;

        [tween animateProperty:@"color" targetValue:SP_RED];
        [Sparrow.juggler addObject:tween];
    }
}
```

9. In the battlefield header file, we need to add an instance variable called _enemyShip, which is a pointer to the class `Ship`.

10. Update the references from `ship` to _enemyShip.

11. Add an event listener to the `SP_EVENT_TYPE_ENTER_FRAME` event, as shown in the following code:

```
[self addEventListener:@selector(onEnterFrame:) atObject:self
    forType:SP_EVENT_TYPE_ENTER_FRAME];
```

12. Implement the `onEnterFrame` method with the following lines of code:

```
-(void) onEnterFrame:(SPEvent *)event
{
  if (_pirateShip.isShooting) {
    SPRectangle *enemyShipBounds = [_enemyShip
      boundsInSpace:self];
    SPRectangle *ball1 = [_pirateShip.cannonBallLeft
      boundsInSpace:self];
    SPRectangle *ball2 = [_pirateShip.cannonBallRight
      boundsInSpace:self];

    if ([enemyShipBounds intersectsRectangle:ball1] ||
      [enemyShipBounds intersectsRectangle:ball2]) {
      if (_pirateShip.cannonBallLeft.visible ||
        _pirateShip.cannonBallRight.visible) {
        [_pirateShip abortShooting];
        [_enemyShip hit];
      }
    }
  }
}
```

13. Run the example. When the enemy ship is hit, it flashes red for a moment, as shown in the following screenshot:

What just happened?

In step 2, we updated our `hitpoints` property so that we can add custom getters and setters. In the next step, we declared the methods `abortShooting` and `hit`. We needed the first method to cancel the current shooting animations and the second method to do something when a ship has been hit.

We defined the custom getter and setter in steps 5 and 6, respectively. For the getter, we just returned the instance variable `_hitpoints` that we declared in step 2. For the setter, we set this instance variable; but when `_hitpoints` equals or was below zero, we hid the ship.

The `abortShooting` method in step 7 set the `_isShooting` instance variable, removed all tweens from the cannonballs, and hid the cannonballs as well.

The `hit` method subtracted 25 points from `hitpoints` and added an animation that let the ship flash red for a very short amount of time to get some visual feedback if a ship had been hit.

In the next two steps, we refactored the enemy ship instance to be an instance variable, instead of being a local variable inside the initializer. We also updated all references to the enemy ship.

In step 11, we added an event listener. This event listener was called on each frame. In the next step, we implemented the collision between the enemy ship and the cannonballs from the pirate ship.

First, we needed to get the bounds from each of these objects relative to the current scene. We needed to see if any of the cannonballs intersected with the enemy ship. In order to make sure that the cannons were actually firing, we checked for the visibility of the cannonballs, and then we called the `hit` method from the enemy ship and the `abortShooting` method from the pirate ship. The latter was necessary, otherwise the check would happen again with a positive result, so much so that the enemy ship would be destroyed instantly and we wouldn't even get to see the red flashing ship.

When we ran the example, we needed to hit the enemy ship exactly four times for it to disappear. Each time the enemy ship was hit, it flashed red for a moment.

Loading gameplay-relevant data

Let's reflect on what kind of gameplay-relevant data we have at this moment. They are:

- Hit points for each ship
- The damage a cannonball inflicts
- Positions for each ship in the battlefield

We should put this data in a file and load it in the game.

Time for action – avoiding hardcoded values

To separate and load our gameplay-relevant data, we need to follow these steps:

1. Add a new file called `gameplay.json` in the `Resources` folder with the following content:

```
{
    "hitpoints": 100,
    "damage": 25,
    "battlefield": {
        "enemy": {
            "x": 100,
            "y": 100
        },
        "pirate": {
            "x": 300,
            "y": 100
        }
    }
}
```

2. Open the `Ship.h` file.

3. Add a property called `maxHitpoints`, as shown in the following line of code:

```
@property int maxHitpoints;
```

4. Inside the `Ship` initializer, replace the piece of code where we set `hitpoints` with the following lines of code:

```
self.maxHitpoints = [(NSNumber *) [Assets
   dictionaryFromJSON:@"gameplay.json"][@"hitpoints"] intValue];

self.hitpoints = self.maxHitpoints;
```

5. Inside the `hit` method, replace the hardcoded damage value to load from the `gameplay.json` file, as shown in the following code:

```
self.hitpoints = self.hitpoints - [(NSNumber *) [Assets
   dictionaryFromJSON:@"gameplay.json"][@"damage"] intValue];
```

6. Inside the `Battlefield.m` file, replace the hardcoded ship positions with those from the `gameplay.json` file, as shown in the following code:

```
NSDictionary *gameplayFile = [Assets
   dictionaryFromJSON:@"gameplay.json"];

_pirateShip = [[Ship alloc] initWithType:ShipPirate];
_pirateShip.x = [(NSNumber *)
   gameplayFile[@"battlefield"][@"pirate"][@"x"] floatValue];
_pirateShip.y = [(NSNumber *)
   gameplayFile[@"battlefield"][@"pirate"][@"y"] floatValue];

_enemyShip = [[Ship alloc] init];
_enemyShip.x = [(NSNumber *)
   gameplayFile[@"battlefield"][@"enemy"][@"x"] floatValue];
_enemyShip.y = [(NSNumber *)
   gameplayFile[@"battlefield"][@"enemy"][@"y"] floatValue];
```

7. Run the example.

Instead of having hardcoded values in our code, we are now loading the values from a file. As a result, the ships are at different starting positions, as shown in the following screenshot:

What just happened?

In step 1, we created the JSON file with values that we will load later on. The values we have so far are the hit points, damage, and of course, positions of the ships.

Inside the Ship.h file, we added a new property called maxHitpoints, which indicates the maximum health of any ship.

In step 4, we first set the maxHitpoints property with the hitpoints property from the gameplay.json file. Since a property is loaded from the gameplay.json file and it is from the type id, we need to cast it into a more familiar data type. We casted it into a pointer to NSNumber and then used its integer value through the intValue method.

In the next step, we did the same for the damage property.

In step 6, we switched to the battlefield scene and updated the positions for the ships to reflect the same from the gameplay.json file.

When we ran the example, our ships were at the position we defined in the gameplay.json file. Shooting and destroying an enemy worked as expected.

Pop quiz

Q1. How can event listeners be described?

1. Using blocks

2. Using selectors

3. Using selectors or blocks

Q2. When is an event registered to `SP_TYPE_EVENT_ENTER_FRAME` called?

1. Once in the first frame after it's added to the display tree

2. Once every frame

3. Never

Q3. Detecting double taps is not possible with Sparrow.

1. True

2. False

Summary

In this chapter, we learned about adding the basic game logic elements to our game.

Specifically, we covered how to structure our code. We got a deeper knowledge of touches, event listeners, and collision detections.

Now that our pirate ship can actually shoot and hit things, let's add user-interface elements—which is the topic of the next chapter.

7
User Interface

In the previous chapter, we learned about adding the first gameplay elements into our game. Our pirate ship can now shoot cannonballs, and if the cannonballs hit the enemy enough number of times, the enemy ship will be destroyed.

In this chapter, we are going to add user interface elements. Specifically, we will improve our game in the following aspects:

- ◆ Display and update the health of each ship
- ◆ Add buttons on the screen
- ◆ Display text on the screen

So, let's start by adding a visual representation for hit points on the screen.

Displaying the hit points of each ship

By default, each ship has 100 hit points, and each cannonball does 25 points of damage to those hit points. We do have some visual feedback when a cannonball hits a ship, but we don't know how many hit points a ship has once hit a few times.

Time for action – placing a health bar on top of each ship

To display the hit points for each ship, we just need to follow these steps:

1. Open our game's project file if it's not already open.
2. Switch to the `Ship.h` file.

3. Add an instance variable called `_quadHitpoints`, which is a pointer to `SPQuad`, as shown in the following line of code:

```
SPQuad *_quadHitpoints;
```

4. Switch to the `Ship.m` file. Just after where we create the cannonball images in the initializer, we add a quad which should be the border for our hit point representation, as shown in the following code:

```
float hitpointsHeight = 5.0f;
SPQuad *hitpointsBorder = [SPQuad quadWithWidth:clipNorth.width
  height:hitpointsHeight color:SP_BLACK];
```

5. We add the background for the hit points box, as shown in the following code:

```
uint redColor = SP_COLOR(200, 0, 0);
SPQuad *quadMaxHitpoints = [SPQuad
  quadWithWidth:hitpointsBorder.width - 2.0f
    height:hitpointsHeight - 2.0f color:redColor];
```

6. We set the background for the hit points box to have a one point margin, which means its position needs to be one point to the left and one point up from the local coordinate system:

```
quadMaxHitpoints.x = 1.0f;
quadMaxHitpoints.y = 1.0f;
```

7. We then create `SPQuad` from the `_quadHitpoints` instance variable, as shown in the following code:

```
uint greenColor = SP_COLOR(0, 180, 0);
_quadHitpoints = [SPQuad quadWithWidth:hitpointsBorder.width -
  2.0f height:hitpointsHeight - 2.0f color:greenColor];
```

8. As shown in the following code, we set the hit points to the same coordinates as the background:

```
_quadHitpoints.x = quadMaxHitpoints.x;
_quadHitpoints.y = quadMaxHitpoints.y;
```

9. We then add all of the hit point quads to the display tree, as shown in the following code:

```
[self addChild:hitpointsBorder];
[self addChild:quadMaxHitpoints];
[self addChild:_quadHitpoints];
```

10. Inside the `setHitpoints` method, add the following line of code just after the statement where we set the instance variable to the value of the parameter:

```
_quadHitpoints.scaleX = (float) _hitpoints / self.maxHitpoints;
```

11. Run the example.

As seen in the following screenshot, both ships now have the amount of their hit points represented as red and green bars:

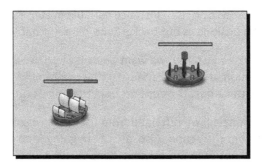

What just happened?

In step 1, we opened our Xcode template from where we had left off in the previous chapter. First of all, we need an instance variable that should represent our hit points. If we think about how other games display the current hit points, in strategy games mostly, the hit points are represented as little green and red bars above each unit. In fighting games, the hit points are displayed at the top left- and right-hand sides for each player. As we might have more than one enemy on the screen, the best representation will be to have red and green bars above each of the ship. The green portion of the bar would be the amount of hit points the ship currently has and the red portion is the amount that is currently missing.

In step 2, we switched to the Ship.h file as we wanted to define an instance variable. To represent the hit points, we chose SPQuad and called our variable _quadHitpoints. To actually implement the hit point mechanics, we switched to the Ship.m file. Our hit points bar actually consists of three different boxes:

- ◆ A border around the hit points
- ◆ The background for the hit points (a red bar)
- ◆ The actual hit point bar (a green bar which is represented by our _quadHitpoints instance variable)

In step 5, we defined a black rectangle that will act as the border for our hit point bar. The width of the rectangle should be the width of the ship. We got the width from the clipNorth movie clip. Actually, we can also get the ship's width from any other movie clips. We set the height of the black rectangle to five points. We don't want the hit points bar to be too thick, but it has to be easily visible and recognizable.

In the next step, we set the background of the hit points. We defined a SPQuad instance, which we call quadMaxHitpoints. It should be one point smaller than the black rectangle on each side. We used the width from the hitpointsBorder instance and had set the height to three points.

We set the left and the top of the `quadMaxHitpoints` instance to one point each so that it will actually look as if the hit point bar has a border.

We then initialized the `quadHitpoints` instance variable in step 8. It's a `SPQuad` class as well and has the same dimensions as our background hit point bar.

With the `quadMaxHitpoints` instance, we want `_quadHitpoints` to be displayed inside the border. So, we set the position of `_quadHitpoints` one point to the left and top relative to the ship itself. In this case, we can adjust the position from the `quadMaxHitpoints` quad.

For the red and green rectangles, we refrained from using bright colors, as this might strain the eyes and distract us from the action. Also, as we are going for a darker tone in general, having bright colors would not fit in this context. Keep in mind when coloring and designing the user interface that the elements should be tested on the actual device. The brightness is usually not at its maximum, especially if the device is running on battery. In some cases, graphics are even given additional contrast or are brightened so that they don't look too dark on mobile devices.

In step 10, we added all of the quads to the display tree; all of the quads are children of the `Ship` class.

After this point, our code snippet will look like the following:

```
SPMovieClip *clipSouthWest = [SPMovieClip
  movieWithFrames:texturesSouthWest fps:animationFPS];
SPMovieClip *clipSouthEast = [SPMovieClip
  movieWithFrames:texturesSouthEast fps:animationFPS];

_shootingClip = [NSArray arrayWithObjects:clipNorth, clipSouth,
  clipWest, clipEast, clipNorthWest, clipNorthEast, clipSouthWest,
    clipSouthEast, nil];

self.cannonBallLeft = [SPImage imageWithTexture:[Assets
  texture:@"cannonball.png"]];
self.cannonBallRight = [SPImage imageWithTexture:[Assets
  texture:@"cannonball.png"]];

float hitpointsHeight = 5.0f;
        SPQuad *hitpointsBorder = [SPQuad quadWithWidth:clipNorth.
          width height:hitpointsHeight color:SP_BLACK];

  uint redColor = SP_COLOR(200, 0, 0);
        SPQuad *quadMaxHitpoints = [SPQuad
          quadWithWidth:hitpointsBorder.width - 2.0f
            height:hitpointsHeight - 2.0f color:redColor];
```

```
        quadMaxHitpoints.x = 1.0f;
        quadMaxHitpoints.y = 1.0f;

    uint greenColor = SP_COLOR(0, 180, 0);
        _quadHitpoints = [SPQuad quadWithWidth:hitpointsBorder.width -
            2.0f height:hitpointsHeight - 2.0f color:greenColor];
        _quadHitpoints.x = quadMaxHitpoints.x;
        _quadHitpoints.y = quadMaxHitpoints.y;

for (SPMovieClip* clip in _shootingClip) {
  clip.loop = NO;
  [self addChild:clip];
}

self.cannonBallLeft.visible = NO;
self.cannonBallRight.visible = NO;

[self addChild:self.cannonBallLeft];
[self addChild:self.cannonBallRight];

[self addChild:hitpointsBorder];
[self addChild:quadMaxHitpoints];
[self addChild:_quadHitpoints];

self.direction = DirectionSouthWest;
```

If we were to use the hit points' creation code more than once, it is considered a best practice to put this piece of code into a separate method.

In the next step, we updated the hit points setter. The _quadHitpoints instance will be scaled horizontally. As both _hitpoints and self.maxHitpoints are integer values, we needed to cast it to a float value. If we don't do this, the hit points bar would either be red or green with nothing in between.

The setHitpoints method will look like the following piece of code after step 10:

```
-(void) setHitpoints:(int)hitpoints
{
    _hitpoints = hitpoints;

    _quadHitpoints.scaleX = (float) _hitpoints / self.maxHitpoints;

    if (_hitpoints <= 0) {
        self.visible = FALSE;
    }
}
```

We ran the example in the last step and saw that the enemy ship as well as our ship have hit point bars on top of them. When the ships moved, the hit point bars also moved with them, and when we hit the enemy ship, the hit points bar updated itself accordingly.

Adding buttons to the screen

Now that we have hit point bars on the screen, let's add some things that the user can actually interact with.

Pausing and resuming the game

The first thing we are going to add is the ability to pause and resume the game at will. This is actually quite important, especially for mobile action games. If a call comes on the mobile device (iPhone) and we don't have a pause functionality, the player might get frustrated by not being able to pause the game and lose their progress or winning streak.

Before we get into implementing these buttons, let's download the necessary graphics for this chapter which are available at `https://github.com/freezedev/pirategame-assets/releases/download/0.7/Graphics_07.zip`. Copy the contents of the extracted file into the project.

Let's think of what we need to do when pausing the game:

- ◆ Display a button to pause the game
- ◆ Display a button to resume the game
- ◆ Stop all current tweens when the player clicks on the pause button
- ◆ Resume all current tweens when the player clicks on the resume button

As this is a bigger task, we are splitting it into two parts; first, we are going to display the buttons, and then we will implement the functionality.

Displaying the pause and resume buttons on the screen

In this example, we are going to add all of the buttons we need and will display them at the correct position on the screen.

Time for action – putting buttons on the screen

To add our first buttons, follow these steps:

1. Open the `Battlefield.h` file.

2. Add one instance variable for each button. We will use the SPButton type, as shown in the following code:

```
SPButton *_buttonPause;
SPButton *_buttonResume;
```

3. Switch to the Battlefield.m file.

4. Construct the instances for our two instance variables, as shown in the following code:

```
_buttonPause = [SPButton buttonWithUpState:[[Assets
   textureAtlas:@"ui.xml"] textureByName:@"button_pause"]];
_buttonResume = [SPButton buttonWithUpState:[[Assets
   textureAtlas:@"ui.xml"] textureByName:@"button_play"]];
```

5. Set the position of both the pause and resume buttons to the top-right corner of the screen using the following code:

```
_buttonPause.x = Sparrow.stage.width - _buttonPause.width -
   4.0f;
_buttonPause.y = 4.0f;

_buttonResume.x = _buttonPause.x;
_buttonResume.y = _buttonPause.y;
```

6. Hide the resume button using the following line of code:

```
_buttonResume.visible = NO;
```

7. For later usage, create methods to tap the pause and resume buttons, as shown in the following code:

```
-(void) onButtonPause:(SPTouchEvent *)event
{

}

-(void) onButtonResume:(SPTouchEvent *)event
{

}
```

8. Bind the newly created methods to the pause and resume buttons, as shown in the following code:

```
[_buttonPause addEventListener:@selector(onButtonPause:)
   atObject:self forType:SP_EVENT_TYPE_TRIGGERED ];
[_buttonResume addEventListener:@selector(onButtonResume:)
   atObject:self forType:SP_EVENT_TYPE_TRIGGERED ];
```

9. Add both buttons to the display tree as follows:

```
[self addChild:_buttonPause];
[self addChild:_buttonResume];
```

10. Run the example to see the result. We now have a pause button on the screen, as shown in the following screenshot:

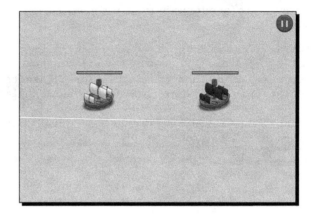

What just happened?

In step 1, we opened the Battlefield.h file. We added two instance variables to this class, one for the pause button and one for the resume button. We used the SPButton class, which is pretty much an image, and optionally displayed some text on top of it.

Next, we switched to the Battlefield.m file. In step 4, we initialized both buttons. We need to take a closer look at the following two points:

- We already know that we can get an array of textures if we use the texturesStartingWith method. If we want only a single texture, we need to use textureByName, and we also have to specify the correct name.

- SPButton provides several factory methods. The one we are using is the buttonWithUpState method in which we have to pass an SPTexture instance. The up state is the texture that is visible all the time. If we were to specify a down state, the down state would be visible once the button is tapped. Another factory method lets us specify either the down state or even some text.

In the next step, we positioned the buttons at the top-right of the screen. We left a bit of space (four points) so that the button is not too close to the edge of the screen.

In step 6, we hid the resume button so that we only see the pause button the first time the scene is being shown.

In the next step, we added some dummy methods to pause and resume the game. We left these empty for now, but we'll fill them in a little bit.

Next, we linked these methods to the buttons so that they will be called when we touch these buttons.

To actually show the buttons on the screen, we need to add them to the display tree, which we did in step 9.

Let's take a look at what exactly changed in the initializer:

```
SPTween *shipTween = [SPTween tweenWithTarget:_enemyShip time:4.0f
  transition:SP_TRANSITION_EASE_IN_OUT];
[shipTween animateProperty:@"y" targetValue:250];
shipTween.repeatCount = 5;
shipTween.reverse = YES;
shipTween.delay = 2.0f;

_buttonPause = [SPButton buttonWithUpState:[[Assets
  textureAtlas:@"ui.xml"] textureByName:@"button_pause"]];
_buttonResume = [SPButton buttonWithUpState:[[Assets
  textureAtlas:@"ui.xml"] textureByName:@"button_play"]];

_buttonPause.x = Sparrow.stage.width - _buttonPause.width - 4.0f;
_buttonPause.y = 4.0f;

_buttonResume.x = _buttonPause.x;
_buttonResume.y = _buttonPause.y;

_buttonResume.visible = NO;

[_buttonPause addEventListener:@selector(onButtonPause:)
  atObject:self forType:SP_EVENT_TYPE_TOUCH];
[_buttonResume addEventListener:@selector(onButtonResume:)
  atObject:self forType:SP_EVENT_TYPE_TOUCH];

[Sparrow.juggler addObject:shipTween];

[_background addEventListener:@selector(onBackgroundTouch:)
  atObject:self forType:SP_EVENT_TYPE_TOUCH];
[_pirateShip addEventListener:@selector(onShipTap:) atObject:self
  forType:SP_EVENT_TYPE_TOUCH];

[self addEventListener:@selector(onEnterFrame:) atObject:self
  forType:SP_EVENT_TYPE_ENTER_FRAME];
```

```
[self addChild:_background];
[self addChild:_enemyShip];
[self addChild:_pirateShip];

[self addChild:_buttonPause];
[self addChild:_buttonResume];
```

Now, when we ran the example, we saw the pause button in the top-right corner of the screen. When we tap the button, nothing happens except for the button scaling down a bit.

Implementing the logic to pause and resume the game

Now that we have displayed the buttons on the screen, let's allow the player to pause and resume the game. We are going to utilize our own juggler and, save if the game is paused into a variable and if the game is not paused, we advance our juggler as well as the child elements.

Time for action – allowing the player to pause and resume

To allow the player to pause and resume the game, we need to follow these steps:

1. Open the `Ship.h` file.

2. Add an instance variable called `_juggler` that is a pointer to `SPJuggler`, as shown in the following line of code:

    ```
    SPJuggler *_juggler;
    ```

3. Declare a property called `paused`, which is of the type `BOOL`, as shown in the following line of code:

    ```
    @property (nonatomic) BOOL paused;
    ```

4. Declare a method called `advanceTime`, as shown in the following line of code:

    ```
    -(void) advanceTime:(double)seconds;
    ```

5. Switch to the `Ship.m` file.

6. Inside the initializer, set the `paused` property to `NO` using its instance variable, as shown in the following code:

    ```
    _isShooting = NO;
    _paused = NO;

    SPTextureAtlas *atlas = (type == ShipPirate) ? [Assets
      textureAtlas:@"ship_pirate_small_cannon.xml"] : [Assets
        textureAtlas:@"ship_small_cannon.xml"];
    ```

7. Initialize the `_juggler` instance variable inside the initializer with the following line of code:

```
_juggler = [SPJuggler juggler];
```

8. Update all references from `Sparrow.juggler` to `_juggler`.

9. Implement the `advanceTime` method with the following lines of code:

```
-(void) advanceTime:(double)seconds
{
    if (!self.paused) {
        [_juggler advanceTime:seconds];
    }
}
```

10. Switch to the `Battlefield.h` file.

11. Add an instance variable for `juggler` here as well:

```
SPJuggler *_juggler;
```

12. Add an instance variable for the background using the following line of code:

```
SPImage *_background;
```

13. Add a property called `paused` which is a `BOOL` type. As we are going to add custom getters and setters for this property, we also need an instance variable called `_paused` as shown in the following code:

```
@interface Battlefield : Scene {
    Ship *_pirateShip;
    Ship *_enemyShip;

    SPImage *_background;

    SPButton *_buttonPause;
    SPButton *_buttonResume;

    SPJuggler *_juggler;

    BOOL _paused;
}

@property (nonatomic) BOOL paused;
```

14. Switch to the `Battlefield.m` file.

15. Inside the initializer, update the reference from the local background variable to the `_background` instance variable.

16. Inside the `Battlefield` initializer, initialize the `_juggler` instance. This has to be done before we add `shipTween` to `juggler`:

```
[_buttonPause addEventListener:@selector(onButtonPause:)
  atObject:self forType:SP_EVENT_TYPE_TOUCH];
[_buttonResume addEventListener:@selector(onButtonResume:)
  atObject:self forType:SP_EVENT_TYPE_TOUCH];

_juggler = [SPJuggler juggler];

[Sparrow.juggler addObject:shipTween];
```

17. Update all references from `Sparrow.juggler` to `_juggler`.

18. Add a custom setter for the `paused` property with the following content:

```
- (void) setPaused:(BOOL)paused
{
    _paused = paused;

    _buttonResume.visible = _paused;
    _buttonPause.visible = !_paused;

    _background.touchable = !_paused;

    _pirateShip.paused = _paused;
    _enemyShip.paused = _paused;
}
```

19. Add a custom getter for the `paused` property that returns the `_paused` instance variable:

```
- (BOOL) paused
{
    return _paused;
}
```

20. Implement the `onButtonPause` and `onButtonResume` methods by setting the `paused` property to its correct values (`YES` in the `onButtonPause` method, `NO` in the `onButtonResume` method).

21. Update the parameter type in `onEnterFrame` from being a pointer to `SPEvent` to being a pointer to `SPEnterFrameEvent`.

22. Add the following lines of code to the `onEnterFrame` method:

```
double passedTime = event.passedTime;

[_enemyShip advanceTime:passedTime];
[_pirateShip advanceTime:passedTime];
```

```
if (!self.paused) {
  [_juggler advanceTime:passedTime];
}
```

23. Run the example.

We can now tap the pause and resume buttons. In the following screenshot, you can see that when the game is paused, all animations stop until we press the resume button:

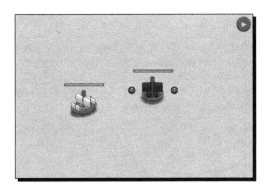

What just happened?

In the Ship.h file, we updated the interface by performing the following tasks:

- Added a new juggler instance variable, which is a pointer to SPJuggler (step 2)
- Added a paused property with the type BOOL (step 3)
- Declared a method called advanceTime (step 4)

Sparrow does not provide the pause and resume methods for its jugglers. We dealt with this by introducing our own jugglers and setting a flag if the game is paused, and we advanced all of our jugglers only if the game was not paused.

In step 5, we switched to the Ship.m file and we defined the paused property inside the initializer to NO, because by default, the ships should not be paused. This step is not necessary as Objective-C initializes this instance as NO; it's just a reminder to see which instance variables we have if we were to decide to change a value later on, and we know where to look.

In the next step, we initialized the _juggler instance variable. It does not matter where exactly we defined the juggler instance variable inside the initializer as we don't add any tweens to jugglers in the initializer method. Next, we searched and replaced all references from Sparrow.juggler to _juggler. The easiest way is to use *command + F*, select **Replace** from the drop-down list, put Sparrow.juggler in the first input box, _juggler in the second input, and select **All** to replace all the references.

In step 9, we implemented the `advanceTime` method, where we call the `advanceTime` method from `_juggler` and pass in `double` as the `seconds` parameter. This is only called if the `paused` property is set to `NO`.

Next, we switched to the `Battlefield.h` file. Here, we needed to perform the following steps:

- Add an instance variable for a juggler, similar to how we did for the `Ship` class (step 11).
- We now need an instance variable that references the background image instance (step 12).
- We need a `paused` property. As we are going to implement custom getters and setters, we also need an instance variable corresponding to that property (step 13).

Then, we switched to the `Battlefield.m` file. In the next step, we updated all references from the local background variable to the instance variable `_background`.

In step 16, we initialized our `_juggler` instance variable. Here, it does matter where we initialize this instance; it should be right before the line `[Sparrow.juggler addObject:shipTween];`.

Next, we updated the references to use `_juggler` instead of `Sparrow.juggler` inside the battlefield scene.

Then, we defined the setter for the `paused` property. Let's take a closer look at what exactly happened:

- We set the `_paused` instance variable to the value of the parameter.
- If `_paused` is set to `YES`, `_buttonPause` is not visible and `_buttonResume` is visible. If `_paused` is set to `NO`, it's the other way round.
- Each sprite has a `touchable` property. If this is set to `NO`, touch handlers won't fire. We set this to `NO` so the game can be paused.
- We paused all ships on the screen.

In step 19, we defined the getter for the `paused` property. It just returned the `_paused` instance variable.

We then implemented the `onButtonPause` and `onButtonResume` methods, where we set the `paused` property to `YES` and `NO`, respectively.

In step 21, we needed to update the parameter type in our `onEnterFrame` method. It needs to be a pointer to `SPEnterFrame`.

Then, we added some lines of code to the `onEnterFrame` method. Now that the event is a pointer to `SPEnterFrame`, we can actually get the time that has been passed by getting the `passedTime` property from the event parameter. We then called the `advanceTime` method from all the ships on the screen, and if the scene is paused, we call the `advanceTime` method from `_juggler`.

When we ran the example, we can now pause and resume the game at will.

Have a go hero

Here are some suggestions of what we could improve:

- As there isn't much happening in the `onButtonPause` and `onButtonResume` methods, we could either try to use blocks or merge both methods into one.

- We could extend the `Scene` class to use a `juggler` instance variable, so we don't need to redefine a custom juggler wherever we need it.

- Right now, we have custom user interface elements for each scene. However, if this were to change, we should think about abstracting the user interface logic into a separate class and maybe bind it to the `Scene` class.

Aborting the current game

So far, we don't have the ability to switch to the pirate cove scene. However, we should introduce the option to abort the current fight.

Time for action – conceding the game

To abort the current game, we need to follow these steps:

1. Open the `Battlefield.m` file.

2. Inside the initializer, we should add the abort button right after the resume button:

```
SPButton *buttonAbort = [SPButton buttonWithUpState:[[Assets
    textureAtlas:@"ui.xml"] textureByName:@"button_abort"]];
```

3. Position the abort button in the bottom-right corner:

```
buttonAbort.x = Sparrow.stage.width - buttonAbort.width - 4.0f;
buttonAbort.y = Sparrow.stage.height - buttonAbort.height -
    4.0f;
```

4. Import the `SceneDirector` class, as shown in the following line of code:

```
#import "SceneDirector.h"
```

5. Add a listener to the abort button using a block, as shown in the following code:

```
[buttonAbort addEventListenerForType:SP_EVENT_TYPE_TRIGGERED
  block:^(SPEvent *event)
{
  [((SceneDirector *) self.director) showScene:@"piratecove"];
}];
```

6. Add the button to the display tree, as shown in the following code:

```
[self addChild:buttonAbort];
```

7. Run the example to see the result.

We now see the abort button as shown in the following screenshot:

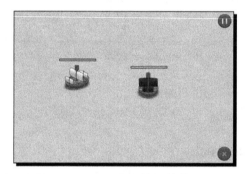

What just happened?

In step 1, we opened the Battlefield.m file. For this example, we only need to take a look at the initializer method. We initialized the abort button similar to how we did for the pause and resume buttons before, the only difference is that we are using a different texture.

In the next step, we positioned the abort button at the bottom-right corner. Just like how we left a bit of space with the pause and resume buttons, we did the same here.

We then imported the SceneDirector.h file in the next step.

In step 5, we added an event listener to the abort button. Inside the event listener, we switched to the pirate cove scene. Although we do have a reference to the scene director using the director property, it is of the type id. So, we needed to recast it to a pointer to the SceneDirector class.

Then, we added the abort button to the display tree.

When we ran the example, we saw the abort button, and when we tapped it, we jumped to the pirate cove scene.

Adding dialogs to the screen

Now that we have added the abort button on the screen, we might run into a few problems, which are as follows:

- We might tap on the abort button by accident
- We don't have any way to get from the pirate cove scene back to the battlefield scene

So, to counteract this, at least on the surface, let's add a dialog which should be shown when we tap the abort button.

Time for action – creating a dialog class

To add dialogs, we need to follow these steps:

1. Add a new group inside the **Classes** folder called **UI**.

2. Inside the **UI** group, add a new Objective-C class called `Dialog`, which derives from `SPSprite`.

3. Implement the dialog initializer with the following lines of code:

```
-(id) init
{
    if ((self = [super init])) {
        SPImage *background = [SPImage
          imageWithTexture:[[Assets textureAtlas:@"ui.xml"]
            textureByName:@"dialog"]];

        SPButton *buttonYes = [SPButton
          buttonWithUpState:[[Assets textureAtlas:@"ui.xml"]
            textureByName:@"dialog_yes"] text:@"Yes"];

        SPButton *buttonNo = [SPButton
          buttonWithUpState:[[Assets textureAtlas:@"ui.xml"]
            textureByName:@"dialog_no"] text:@"No"];

        buttonYes.x = 24.0f;
        buttonYes.y = background.height - buttonYes.height -
          40.0f;

        buttonNo.x = buttonYes.x + buttonYes.width - 20.0f;
        buttonNo.y = buttonYes.y;

        [self addChild:background];
        [self addChild:buttonYes];
```

```
        [self addChild:buttonNo];
    }

    return self;
}
```

4. Switch to the `Battlefield.m` file.

5. Import the `Dialog.h` file.

6. Right before the abort button event, initialize the dialog, as shown in the following code:

```
Dialog *dialog = [[Dialog alloc] init];

dialog.x = (Sparrow.stage.width - dialog.width) / 2;
dialog.y = (Sparrow.stage.height - dialog.height) / 2;
```

7. The dialog should be hidden by default, as shown in the following line of code:

```
dialog.visible = NO;
```

8. Update the abort button event to show the dialog:

```
[buttonAbort addEventListenerForType: SP_EVENT_TYPE_TRIGGERED
    block:^(SPEvent *event)
{
    dialog.visible = YES;
}];
```

9. Run the example to see the result.

When we tap the abort button, we now see a dialog popping up:

What just happened?

First, we structured the `Dialog` class. To keep it separate from the game logic code, we created it within a new group. The `Dialog` class itself should inherit from `SPSprite`.

In step 3, we defined the initializer for the `Dialog` class, where we performed the following actions:

♦ We added a background image for the dialog.

♦ We added the **Yes** and **No** buttons. We called the factory methods for `SPButton`, where we put some text on the buttons, which in our case is **Yes** and **No**, respectively.

♦ We positioned these elements at the bottom of the dialog.

Inside the `Battlefield.m` file, we imported the `Dialog.h` file to be able to use the `Dialog` class.

Inside the initializer of the battlefield scene, we needed to initialize the dialog, which we did right before the abort button event.

We set the dialog to be invisible by default and updated the abort button event to show the dialog.

When we ran the example, we saw the dialog when we tapped the abort button.

Have a go hero

Having the abort button on the bottom-right of the screen is not ideal from a usability point of view. If we accidently tapped the button, a dialog is now being shown instead of just aborting the current battle. Still, it doesn't seem to be ideal. The following are some suggestions on how to improve the situation:

♦ Placing the abort button (`buttonAbort`) next to the pause button. All user interface elements would be in the same area.

♦ Combine the pause button and the abort button into a game menu button. Clicking on the button will pause the game and will open a menu. An abort button can be found there.

Adding custom events to the dialogs

Now that a dialog is on the screen, we would like to attach listeners to the dialog buttons themselves. While we can go for simply attaching touch events, Sparrow provides a way to define custom events.

Time for action – adding our own buttons to our dialog

To add custom events for our dialogs, we just need to follow these steps:

1. Inside the `Dialog.h` file, we need to define the event names before the interface declaration:

```
#define EVENT_TYPE_YES_TRIGGERED @"yesTriggered"
#define EVENT_TYPE_NO_TRIGGERED  @"noTriggered"
```

2. Switch to `Dialog.m`.

3. Register the following listeners to our buttons:

```
[buttonYes addEventListener:@selector(onButtonYes:)
  atObject:self forType:SP_EVENT_TYPE_TRIGGERED];


[buttonNo addEventListener:@selector(onButtonNo:) atObject:self
  forType:SP_EVENT_TYPE_TRIGGERED];
```

4. Implement the `onButtonYes` and `onButtonNo` methods, as shown in the following code:

```
- (void)onButtonYes:(SPEvent *)event
{
    SPEvent *localEvent = [SPEvent
      eventWithType:EVENT_TYPE_YES_TRIGGERED];
    [self dispatchEvent:localEvent];
}

- (void)onButtonNo:(SPEvent *)event
{
    SPEvent *localEvent = [SPEvent
      eventWithType:EVENT_TYPE_NO_TRIGGERED];
    [self dispatchEvent:localEvent];
}
```

5. Switch to `Battlefield.m`.

6. The local dialog variable inside the initializer needs to be refactored into an instance variable called `_dialogAbort`.

7. Move the `#import "Dialog.h"` statement from `Battlefield.m` to `Battlefield.h`.

8. Add event listeners for both dialog buttons in `Battlefield.m`, as shown in the following code:

```
[_dialogAbort addEventListener:@selector(onDialogAbortYes:)
  atObject:self forType:EVENT_TYPE_YES_TRIGGERED];
[_dialogAbort addEventListener:@selector(onDialogAbortNo:)
  atObject:self forType:EVENT_TYPE_NO_TRIGGERED];
```

9. Implement the corresponding methods, as shown in the following code:

```
-(void) onDialogAbortYes:(SPEvent *)event
{
    [((SceneDirector *) self.director)
      showScene:@"piratecove"];
}

-(void) onDialogAbortNo:(SPEvent *)event
{
    self.paused = NO;
    _dialogAbort.visible = NO;
}
```

10. Update the abort button event to also pause the game when the dialog is being shown:

```
[buttonAbort addEventListenerForType:SP_EVENT_TYPE_TOUCH
  block:^(SPEvent *event)
{
  self.paused = YES;
  _dialogAbort.visible = YES;
}];
```

11. Run the example to see the result. When we tap the abort button, we can now tap the buttons of the dialog:

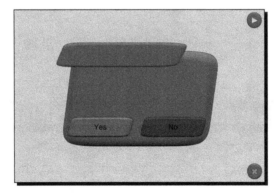

What just happened?

In the first step, we defined the event names for our buttons. In the `Dialog.m` file, we needed to add listeners for our dialog. We used `SP_EVENT_TYPE_TRIGGERED`, so if any kind of event is triggered on either of the buttons, the selector will be called.

In step 4, we implemented the necessary methods. We created an event with our custom event type and dispatched this event afterwards.

In the next step, we refactored the local dialog variable in the battlefield initializer. It now needs to be an instance variable called `_dialogAbort` and it is still a pointer to `Dialog`. We updated all references and the initialization part of the instance variable. Consequently, we imported a statement to the header file.

We then called the `addEventListener` method on our dialog using our custom events.

In step 9, we implemented the methods that should be fired when the button is tapped. If we select **Yes**, we need to show the pirate cove scene, and if we select **No**, we need the dialog to disappear. We also resume the game in this case.

As we resume the game if we tap **Yes**, we also need to update the abort button event to actually pause the game once the dialog is being shown.

When we ran the example and tapped the abort button, our dialog pops up and the game pauses. If we tap **No**, the dialog closes and the game resumes. If we tap **Yes**, we shift to the pirate cove scene.

Drawing text on the screen

There are two ways to display text on the screen. We can either use one of the iOS fonts (so-called system fonts) or we could try to create a more customized font that fits our needs better.

Displaying our first text field

We already drew some text on the screen utilizing the capabilities of `SPButton` when we added the dialog buttons. However, we are now going to draw some text on the screen for the dialog message.

Time for action – adding a text field to the dialog

To draw text on the screen, we need to follow these steps:

1. As shown in the following line of code, add a property called `content`, which is a pointer to `SPTextField`, inside the `Dialog.h` file:

```
@property SPTextField *content;
```

2. In the `Dialog` initializer, create the following content instance and position it between the title box and the buttons:

```
_content = [SPTextField textFieldWithWidth:background.width -
    48.0f height:background.height - 150.0f text:@"Dialog default
        text"];
_content.x = 24.0f;
_content.y = 50.0f;
```

3. Add the `content` property to the display tree, as shown in the following code:

```
[self addChild:background];
[self addChild:buttonYes];
[self addChild:buttonNo];
[self addChild:_content];
```

4. Switch to the `Battlefield.m` file.

5. Add a custom message for the abort dialog, as shown in the following code:

```
_dialogAbort = [[Dialog alloc] init];

_dialogAbort.content.text = @"Would you like to abort the
    current fight?";

_dialogAbort.x = (Sparrow.stage.width - _dialogAbort.width) /
    2;
_dialogAbort.y = (Sparrow.stage.height - _dialogAbort.height) /
    2;
```

6. Run the example.

Now, we see the text message inside the dialog.

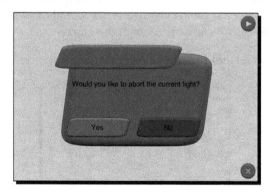

What just happened?

First of all, we needed a property for the message we are going to display. A SPTextField class works like this: we define a rectangle and some text, and the text will automatically be aligned inside the bounds of the rectangle. By default, the text is centered horizontally and vertically. If we want to change this, we need to change the hAlign and vAlign properties to our desired values. In addition to all of the properties it inherits from being a display object (such as color or scale), a text field also has the fontName property to use different fonts and the fontSize property for the size of the text.

In step 2, we created the _content instance, where the text field should be a bit smaller than the dialog itself. We gave the text field a default text and then updated its position to be more or less in the center of the dialog.

After we added the text field to the display tree in step 3, we updated the default message, a custom one, inside the Battlefield initializer.

When we ran the example, we saw our custom message in the dialog.

Explaining system fonts

System fonts are the fonts iOS has built-in, out of the box. The selection ranges from Arial and Helvetica to Verdana, including the light, bold, and italic variants. For a complete list of all available system fonts, visit http://iosfonts.com/.

Explaining bitmap fonts

A bitmap font is very similar to a texture atlas; every character is an image. All of these smaller images are put into a big one. Although system fonts can display Unicode characters with ease, if we need umlauts or similar characters, we would need to add them ourselves. As a result, this would directly increase the size of the image.

A sample bitmap font would look like the following screenshot:

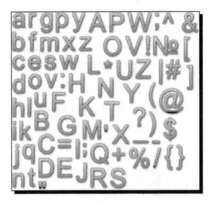

A portion of the data might look something like the following portion of code:

```xml
<font>
  <info face="Arial" size="72" bold="0" italic="0" charset=""
    unicode="" stretchH="100" smooth="1" aa="1" padding="2,2,2,2"
      spacing="0,0" outline="0"/>
  <common lineHeight="83" base="65" scaleW="1024" scaleH="512"
    pages="1" packed="0"/>
  <pages>
    <page id="0" file="font.png"/>
  </pages>
  <chars count="80">
    <char id="97" x="2" y="2" width="45" height="50" xoffset="-1"
      yoffset="18" xadvance="40" page="0" chnl="15"/>
    <char id="98" x="2" y="54" width="44" height="64" xoffset="1"
      yoffset="5" xadvance="40" page="0" chnl="15"/>
    <char id="99" x="2" y="120" width="43" height="50" xoffset="-1"
      yoffset="18" xadvance="36" page="0" chnl="15"/>
    <char id="100" x="2" y="172" width="44" height="64" xoffset="-2"
      yoffset="5" xadvance="40" page="0" chnl="15"/>
    <char id="101" x="47" y="120" width="46" height="50" xoffset="-1"
      yoffset="18" xadvance="40" page="0" chnl="15"/>
    <char id="102" x="48" y="54" width="33" height="64" xoffset="-3"
      yoffset="4" xadvance="20" page="0" chnl="15"/>
    <char id="103" x="83" y="2" width="44" height="65" xoffset="-2"
      yoffset="18" xadvance="40" page="0" chnl="15"/>
    <char id="104" x="2" y="238" width="42" height="63" xoffset="1"
      yoffset="5" xadvance="40" page="0" chnl="15"/>
```

Similar to a texture atlas, the actual data is represented in XML.

There are multiple tools to create bitmap fonts, with each of them having their own advantages and disadvantages. Littera is a free online tool available at `http://kvazars.com/littera/` (requires Adobe Flash Player); other popular commercial solutions are **Glyph Designer** by 71squared and **bmGlyph** by Stéphane Queraud.

Creating our very own bitmap font

For this example, we will use bmGlyph, as it allows us to create multiple scaled bitmap fonts similar to the mechanic `TexturePacker` provides. The bmGlyph solution is available on the Mac App Store at `https://itunes.apple.com/us/app/bmglyph/id490499048?mt=12` for $9.99 or your regional equivalent.

If you don't want to use bmGlyph, the complete bitmap font is also included in the graphics package.

Time for action – using bmGlyph to create a bitmap font

To create our first bitmap font, we just need to follow these steps:

1. Open **bmGlyph**.

2. Select **Arial Rounded MT Bold** as the font.

3. Set **Font size** to **72** points.

4. Scroll down to the **Color Tools** section and check **Shadow**.

5. In the **Shadow** pane, set the **x** property to **2**, the **y** property to **-2**, and the **radius** to **8**.

6. In the **Fill Mode** section, select a brown-yellowish color and select the **Glossy** checkbox.

7. Hit the **Publish** button.

8. In the **Default** target, enter `PirateFont` as the **File Name** and font name (**Force Font Name**). In the **Suffix** input box, add `@4x`.

9. Click on the **50** button inside the **Duplicate with scale** box and add the suffix `@2x`.

10. Click on the **25** button.

11. Select **Sparrow** in the **Format** drop-down list.

12. Make sure that **PirateFont** is displayed in all of the targets as the **File Name** and in **Force Font Name**.

13. Hit **Publish** and then the **Close** button.

    After these steps, we should see the following screen:

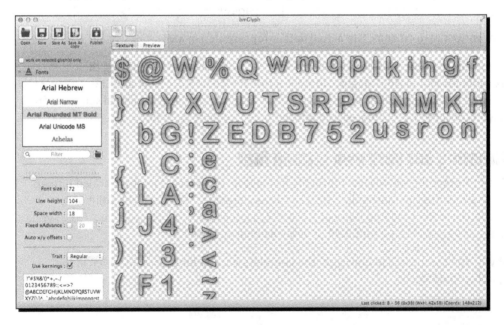

What just happened?

After we opened **bmGlyph**, we set the base font, size, color, and the shadow of the bitmap font. To export the bitmap font, we clicked on the **Publish** button, which we did in step 7. For each separate image, we need to define a new target with a scale. In our case, this is `100%`, `50%`, and `25%` with the suffixes `@4x` and `@2x`, respectively. For the `25%` target, we don't need a suffix.

To export a Sparrow-compatible bitmap font, we needed to select the **Sparrow** format. We needed to make sure that `PirateFont` is written in both **File Name** and **Force Font Name**. If we don't do the latter, the font won't become available as `PirateFont`, but will replace **Arial Rounded MT Bold**.

When we hit the **Publish** button, our font files became available in the location where we wanted to save them.

Displaying a text field with bitmap fonts

Now that we have displayed a system in our dialog, let's display text using our fresh bitmap font as the dialog's title.

Time for action – using our bitmap font for a text field

Follow these steps to display bitmap fonts in `SPTextField`:

1. We need to add another property called `title` inside the `Dialog.h` file, which is also a pointer to `SPTextField`:

   ```
   @property SPTextField *title;
   ```

2. We register our bitmap font, as shown in the following code:

   ```
   [SPTextField registerBitmapFontFromFile:@"PirateFont.fnt"];
   ```

3. We create and position the `_title` instance with the following lines of code:

   ```
   _title = [SPTextField textFieldWithWidth:background.width * 0.6
     height:30.0f text:@"Dialog"];
   _title.fontName = @"PirateFont";
   _title.color = SP_WHITE;

   _title.x = 24.0f;
   _title.y = 26.0f;
   ```

4. We need to add the `_title` instance to the display tree, as shown in the following code:

```
[self addChild:background];
[self addChild:buttonYes];
[self addChild:buttonNo];
[self addChild:_content];
[self addChild:_title];
```

5. Inside the `Battlefield.m` file, we replace the default title with a custom one:

```
_dialogAbort = [[Dialog alloc] init];

_dialogAbort.title.text = @"Abort this fight?";
_dialogAbort.content.text = @"Would you like to abort the
  current fight?";

_dialogAbort.x = (Sparrow.stage.width - _dialogAbort.width) /
  2;
_dialogAbort.y = (Sparrow.stage.height - _dialogAbort.height) /
  2;
```

6. Run the example to see the result.

Our dialog now has a message and a title:

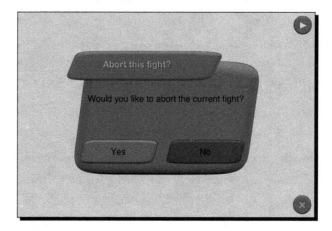

What just happened?

Displaying bitmap fonts is very similar to displaying system fonts on the screen. Before we can use any bitmap font, we need to register it first. When we want to display a text field with this font, we need to update the `fontName` property to reflect the name of the bitmap font.

Another thing to consider is that Sparrow displays all text in black by default. We need to change this in order to see the color effect of our bitmap font.

 Remember that the complete source code for this chapter can also be found on GitHub: `https://github.com/freezedev/pirategame/tree/f742f6026e9ad129546d17e5d9e9728c27ff0733`.

Pop quiz

Q1. In order for custom jugglers to show their tweens, which method needs to be called?

1. `advanceTime`
2. `update`
3. `addJuggler`

Q2. Are bitmap fonts similar to texture atlases?

1. Yes
2. No

Q3. What kind of fonts can be used with `SPTextField`?

1. System fonts
2. Bitmap fonts
3. Both

Summary

In this chapter, we learned about adding user interface elements to the screen.

Specifically, we covered health bars, buttons, and drawing text on the screen, and we got a deeper knowledge of jugglers and how to update elements through custom getters and setters.

Now that we have a basic user interface, let's add some artificial intelligence—which is the topic of the next chapter.

8
Artificial Intelligence and Game Progression

In the previous chapter, we learned about adding user interface elements to our game. We added a hit points representation above our ships, added buttons, and even created our own dialog.

In this chapter, we will add artificial intelligence to our game. The following are the topics we will cover:

- The concepts of fuzzy logic and state machines
- Enemy ships should move and attack
- Adding some kind of progression to the game
- Winning and losing the game

However, before we get to the actual coding, let's see the concepts of artificial intelligence that we will implement.

Artificial intelligence in theory

The goal for the enemy ships is to move around and attack our ships if they get close enough. There are two concepts we need to look into in detail to help us implement this logic; we will discuss these in the following sections.

Explaining fuzzy logic

Let's take a moving train as an example. We could use a Boolean value to describe its state. If it is set to true, it's moving fast; if it's set to false, it's not moving fast.

However, that will not be enough. Let's say the train is moving at 80 miles per hour and then at 100 miles per hour. At both speeds, our Boolean value will be true, but we have no way of differentiating it further. Also, we don't have a state if the train is not moving.

Fuzzy logic describes an interval of values put into a colloquial term. Let's take a step back and compare it to mathematical logic. Binary (two-valued) logic has two values: true and false. An expression such as *1 + 1 = 2* evaluates to "true". The expression "Adding one to one is most likely going to be two" will not make much sense in binary logic, but it will be possible in fuzzy logic.

Fuzzy logic doesn't have the two values true and false, but it has in-between values such as a bit, quite, or about. This is similar to human thinking.

To illustrate this point further, let's take a look at what our moving train example looks like if put in table form:

Term	Speed
Not moving	0 miles per hour
Really slow	1 to 9 miles per hour
Almost fast	10 to 49 miles per hour
Quite fast	50 to 89 miles per hour
Really fast	90 to 119 miles per hour

For our game, we can apply this to a similar value: the distance between the enemy ship and our own ship.

Explaining state machines

State machines are a number of states put into a sequential logic circuit. This sounds abstract, so let's explain it in detail: a state, first of all, is a value that changes if a different state becomes active. A door has two states: locked and unlocked. If the door is locked, it stays locked until it's unlocked.

Here is an example that is closer to our game: we need a number of states, for example, **Move to player**, **Wait 3 seconds**, and **Attack player**.

Now, we need to put these states in some kind of order. Let's say the enemy first moves to the player, and then it attacks and waits for 3 seconds. Then, the process starts again, as demonstrated in the following diagram:

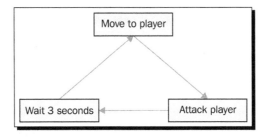

So far, we know about states and state machines. Finite state machines are state machines with a finite number of states. The preceding figure is of course a simplified example of how finite state machines can work. Some of the models also have transitions to describe the action taken to move from one state to another. In illustrations, transitions are often accompanied by conditions such as "Is the player in sight?"

Most simple AIs employ this strategy. One of the most prominent examples is **Quake**. To be fair, different AI mechanics are used in more complex and modern games. One example is the AI adapting to the player's actions: if in a strategy game, the player chooses to attack a specific point, the AI would adapt to defend this position more and more depending on how often the player attacked.

For our purposes, a finite state machine is more than enough. So, let's see what states we need for the enemy ship:

- We want the enemy ship to wander around
- We want the enemy ship to move to the vicinity of the player
- We want the enemy ship to attack
- We want the enemy ship to wait a bit after an attack (for the player to recuperate)

Let's put these states into a diagram as follows:

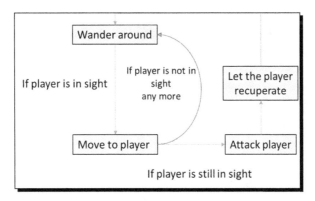

Letting the enemy ship move and attack

Now that we know about fuzzy logic and state machines, we can implement these as mechanics for our artificial intelligence.

Moving the ship

First of all, we want the ship to move around—both wander around and move to the player ship.

Time for action – getting the enemy ship to move around

In order for the enemy ship to move around, we need to use the following steps:

1. Open our Xcode project if it's not already open.

2. Open the `Battlefield.h` file.

3. Define all AI states as `enum`, as shown in the following code:

```
typedef NS_ENUM(NSInteger, AIState) {
    StateWanderAround,
    StateMoveToPlayer,
    StateAttack,
    StateRecuperate
};
```

4. Inside the `Battlefield` scene, add a new instance variable called `_aiState`, which is of the `AIState` type.

5. Open the `Ship.h` file.

6. Add a callback block type, as shown in the following line of code:

```
typedef void(^ShipCallback)(void);
```

7. Declare three new methods for the `Ship` class, as shown in the following code:

```
-(void) moveToX:(float)x andY:(float)y withBlock:(ShipCallback)
   block;
-(float) checkDistanceToShip:(Ship *)ship;
-(void) moveToShip:(Ship *)ship withBlock:(ShipCallback) block;
```

8. Open the `Ship.m` file.

9. Move the contents of the `-(void) moveToX:(float) x andY:(float) y` method into the `-(void) moveToX:(float)x andY:(float)y withBlock:(ShipCallback) block` method.

10. Inside the new `moveTo` method, add the following code just after the
`[tweenY animateProperty:@"y" targetValue:targetY];` line:

```
__block BOOL isTweenXCompleted = NO;
__block BOOL isTweenYCompleted = NO;

tweenX.onComplete = ^{
  isTweenXCompleted = YES;

  if (isTweenXCompleted && isTweenYCompleted) {
    if (block != nil) {
      [block invoke];
    }
  }
};

tweenY.onComplete = ^{
  isTweenYCompleted = YES;

  if (isTweenXCompleted && isTweenYCompleted) {
    if (block != nil) {
      [block invoke];
    }
  }
};
```

11. Implement the `checkDistanceToShip` method with the following code:

```
-(float) checkDistanceToShip:(Ship *)ship
{
SPPoint* p1 = [SPPoint pointWithX:self.x + (self.width / 2)
  y:self.y + (self.height / 2)];
SPPoint* p2 = [SPPoint pointWithX:ship.x + (ship.width / 2)
  y:ship.y + (ship.height / 2)];

float distance = [SPPoint distanceFromPoint:p1 toPoint:p2];

return distance;
}
```

12. The `moveToShip` method should have the following body:

```
-(void) moveToShip:(Ship *)ship withBlock:(ShipCallback)block
{
    floatrandomX = arc4random_uniform(80) - 40.0f;
    floatrandomY = arc4random_uniform(80) - 40.0f;

    [self moveToX:ship.x + randomX andY:ship.y + randomY
        withBlock:block];
}
```

13. Reimplement the `moveToX:(float)x andY:(float)y` method, as shown in the following code:

```
-(void) moveToX:(float)x andY:(float)y
{
    [self moveToX:x andY:y withBlock: nil];
}
```

14. Move on to the `Battlefield.m` file.

15. Inside the initializer, set the `_aiState` instance variable to `StateWanderAround`, as shown in the following line of code:

```
_aiState = StateWanderAround;
```

16. Remove the tween and the juggler.

17. Let's declare a helper method for getting a random position on the screen, as shown in the following code:

```
-(SPPoint *) randomPos
{
    return [SPPoint pointWithX:((arc4random() % (int)
        (Sparrow.stage.width - 80.0f)) + 40.0f) y:((arc4random() %
            (int) (Sparrow.stage.height - 80.0f)) + 40.0f)];
}
```

18. Define a method called `updateAI`, as shown in the following code:

```
-(void) updateAI: (Ship *)ship withState: (AIState) aiState
{
switch (aiState) {
caseStateWanderAround: {
SPPoint *point = [self randomPos];
            [ship moveToX:point.x andY:point.y withBlock:^{
if ([ship checkDistanceToShip:_pirateShip] < 200.0f) {
                //In sight
                [self updateAI:ship
withState:StateMoveToPlayer];
```

```
                    } else {
                        //Not in sight
                        [self updateAI:ship withState:aiState]
                    }
                }];
            }
    break;
    caseStateMoveToPlayer: {
                [ship moveToShip:_pirateShip WithBlock:^{
    if ([ship checkDistanceToShip:_pirateShip] < 100.0f) {
                        // Attack
                        [self updateAI:ship withState:StateAttack];
                    } else {
                        //Not in sight
                        [self updateAI:ship
                          withState:StateWanderAround];
                    }
                }];
            }
    break;
    default:
    break;
        }
}
```

19. Call the `updateAI` method at the point where we initialized the juggler previously, as shown in the following code:

```
[self updateAI:_enemyShip withState:_aiState];
```

20. Run the example.

We now see that our own ship and the enemy ship are moving around on their own.

What just happened?

In step 1, we opened our game project; in the next step, we looked into the `Battlefield.h` file. All of the AI states we previously mentioned were put into `enum`. In step 4, we defined an instance variable that holds the default AI state.

We already had a `moveTo` method in our `Ship` class which lets us move any ship around on the screen. Unfortunately, we currently don't have a way of knowing when the movement is over. We can employ an Objective-C language feature which we used in the previous chapters, that is, blocks. We defined a block as a parameter; when the movement was over, the block was called. In step 6, we defined our block type.

In the next step, we declared the general methods for our `Ship` class:

- Moving to a position and using a callback once the movement is done
- Checking the distance between the current ship and any other ship
- Moving to another ship and using a callback once the operation is over

We then got ready to implement these methods in step 8. We first moved the contents of the old `moveTo` method to the new one with the callback.

Then, we just needed to call the callback block once the animation was over. Since the tweens could potentially have two different speeds depending on the distance between the touch point and the ship, we needed to record whether each tween was completed for both of the tweens. To check if the tween was actually complete, we added a block to the `onComplete` property of the tween. Once the tween was done, the block got called. Inside this block, we set a Boolean value to flag that the current tween was complete, and if both tweens are complete, we invoked the callback. To be able to use our local variables in the `onComplete` blocks, we needed to prefix them with `__blocks`.

In step 11, we implemented a method that calculates the distance between two ships: we took the center of both ships, converted them into `SPPoint`, and utilized the static `distanceFromPoint` method that `SPPoint` provides. We only needed to return the result.

The `moveToShip` method called the `moveTo` method with the coordinates of the ship passed in and some randomness attached to it. We used the `arc4random` function to get a random value. The `arc4random` function returned a floating point number between zero and one. The `arc4random_uniform` function took a parameter and created a random number between zero and the passed-in parameter minus one. In step 13, the `moveTo` method without the callback just called the `moveTo` version, with the callback passing through `nil` as the callback parameter.

When we moved to the `Battlefield.m` file, we set the `_aiState` instance variable to the `WanderState` AI state. We then safely removed the tween and the juggler, which were previously responsible for the enemy ships' move animation.

In step 17, we implemented a method that gets us a random position on the screen. We also set a margin so that the position was definitely within the borders of the screen. We used the SPPoint class factory method to store both the x and y positions.

In the next step, we implemented the method that updates the AI:

♦ If the ship is wandering around, we get a random position and move there.

♦ If the ship has moved, it checks if the distance between the player and the ship parameter is less than 200 points. The ship then moves to the player. If that's not the case, we call the updateAI method again with the WanderState AI state.

♦ If the ship moved to the player, it checks again for the distance. If it's lower than 100 points, it begins attacking, else it's back to wandering around.

Inside the initializer, we called the updateAI method with the enemy ship and our default AI state. This should be right where we previously initialized our instance variable _juggler.

When we ran the example, the enemy ship moved around if it was in the correct state. It moved to the player ship if it was in sight. If the enemy ship was getting too close to the player, it just stopped.

Attacking other ships

Now that the enemy ship is moving around, let's get it to attack our own ship.

Time for action – the enemy should attack the player

For the enemy to attack the players' ship, use the following steps:

1. Open the Ship.h file.

2. Refactor our _juggler instance variable to be a property, as shown in the following line of code:

```
@property SPJuggler *juggler;
```

3. Using the following line of code, add a method called shootWithBlock that should shoot and have a callback as its parameter:

```
-(void) shootWithBlock:(ShipCallback) block;
```

4. Open the Ship.m file and move the contents of the shoot method into the shootWithBlock method.

5. In the shootWithBlock method, invoke the callback as its last statement inside the complete listener of the currentClip variable.

6. Update the shoot method to call the shootWithBlock method with nil.

7. Open the `Battlefield.m` file and add a method for collision detection, as shown in the following code:

```
-(void) checkShipCollision: (Ship *) ship1 againstShip: (Ship *)
ship2
{
    SPRectangle *enemyShipBounds = [ship1 boundsInSpace:self];
    SPRectangle *ball1 = [ship2.cannonBallLeft
      boundsInSpace:self];
    SPRectangle *ball2 = [ship2.cannonBallRight
      boundsInSpace:self];

    if ([enemyShipBounds intersectsRectangle:ball1] ||
      [enemyShipBounds intersectsRectangle:ball2]) {
        if (ship2.cannonBallLeft.visible ||
          ship2.cannonBallRight.visible) {
            [ship2 abortShooting];
            [ship1 hit];
        }
    }
}
```

8. Inside the `onEnterFrame` method, replace the current collision detection with the `checkShipCollision` method, as shown in the following code:

```
[self checkShipCollision:_pirateShipagainstShip:_enemyShip];
[self checkShipCollision:_enemyShipagainstShip:_pirateShip];
```

9. Update the `WanderAround` AI state with an additional attack opportunity, as shown in the following code:

```
if ([ship checkDistanceToShip:_pirateShip] < 200.0f) {
  if ([ship checkDistanceToShip:_pirateShip] < 100.0f) {
    // Attack directly
    [self updateAI:ship withState:StateAttack];
  } else {
    //In sight
    [self updateAI:ship withState:StateMoveToPlayer];
  }
} else {
  //Not in sight
  [self updateAI:ship withState:aiState];
}
```

10. As shown in the following code, add these states to our `switch-case` statements in our `updateAI` method:

```
case StateAttack: {
  [ship shootWithBlock:^{
    [self updateAI:ship withState:StateRecuperate];
  }];
}
case StateRecuperate: {
  [ship.juggler delayInvocationByTime:0.3f block:^{
    [self updateAI:ship withState:StateWanderAround];
  }];
}
```

11. Run the example to see the result.

If the enemy ship gets close enough to our ship and is in the attacking state, it begins to attack our ship. Refer to the following screenshot:

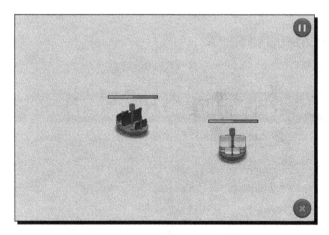

What just happened?

In the `Ship.h` file, we refactored the `_juggler` instance variable into a property since we needed to access it from the battlefield scene and its access should not be limited to a `Ship` instance. We added the `shootWithBlock` method, which we implemented in step 4, where we moved the contents of the `shoot` method to the new `shootWithBlock` method.

We then invoked the callback that should now be the last statement in the event listener where the `currentClip` tween is completed. In step 6, we updated the `shoot` method to call the `shootWithBlock` method with an empty block, just like we did in the previous example.

Since we used collision detection more than once, we put it into a separate method in the next step. Now, we can replace our old collision detection logic by calling the new collision detection. We need to call it twice, once with _pirateShip as the first parameters and _enemyShip as the second parameter. The order of the parameter needs to be the other way around when we call checkShipCollision for the second time.

In step 9, we added an additional state transition. If the distance between the pirate ship and the enemy ship was less than 100 points, it attacked directly instead of moving to the player first. In the following steps, we added the following two missing states:

- In the attack state, we called the shootWithBlock method, and when the shooting was complete, we moved to the recuperating state
- In the StateRecuperate AI state, we waited for 0.3 seconds and then moved on to wandering around

When we ran the example, our state machine was completely finished and all states were being used.

Adding fuzzy values to the AI

Our AI works so far, but we don't have any fuzzy logic yet.

Time for action – spicing up the AI with fuzzy values

To replace our hardcoded values, we need to use the following steps:

1. Open the Battlefield.m file.
2. Add a new method called fuzzyValue, as shown in the following code:

```
-(float) fuzzyValue: (NSString *) value
{
  if ([value isEqualToString:@"Very near"]) {
    return (float) (arg4random() % 40) + 40.0f;
  } else if ([value isEqualToString:@"Quite near"]) {
    result = (float) (arc4random() % 30) + 70.0f;
  } else {
    result = (float) (arc4random() % 50) + 150.0f;
  }
}
```

3. Using the following code, update the hardcoded values with the values from the `fuzzyValue` method:

```
if ([ship checkDistanceToShip:_pirateShip] < [self
    fuzzyValue:@"Near"]) {
if ([ship checkDistanceToShip:_pirateShip] < [self
    fuzzyValue:@"Very near"]) {
if ([ship checkDistanceToShip:_pirateShip] < [self
    fuzzyValue:@"Quite near"]) {
```

4. Run the example. If we were to insert logging to see what the values actually are, we would see the following output:

```
PirateGame[5296:907] Fuzzy value: Near, actual value: 170.000000
PirateGame[5296:907] Fuzzy value: Very near, actual value: 70.000000
PirateGame[5296:907] Fuzzy value: Near, actual value: 199.000000
PirateGame[5296:907] Fuzzy value: Near, actual value: 172.000000
PirateGame[5296:907] Fuzzy value: Very near, actual value: 75.000000
PirateGame[5296:907] Fuzzy value: Quite near, actual value: 95.000000
PirateGame[5296:907] Fuzzy value: Near, actual value: 171.000000
PirateGame[5296:907] Fuzzy value: Near, actual value: 152.000000
```

What just happened?

The goal for this example is to replace our hardcoded values with something that resembles fuzzy logic. In step 2, we added a method that checks against the value and returns a new random value each time. The randomness is not a necessary factor of fuzzy logic, but it is used in this case so that the values are inside a specific range.

If we were to have more fuzzy values, it would be a good idea to hold those values inside `NSDictionary`. This dictionary would have a colloquial term as its key and a block for its value. Inside the block would be logic to return a random number. If the fuzzy value gets passed in, we call the block and get a random number.

Next up, we updated the hardcoded values with the `fuzzyValue` method and put it in a colloquial term each time.

When we ran the example, the AI worked like it did before, but it had additional randomness now.

Have a go hero

We can improve the AI quite a bit by moving the AI logic away from the battlefield scene into a separate class. Since we used the strings for our fuzzy values quite a lot, it may be a good idea to move them into constants or even create our own macros.

Adding progression to our game

Now that our AI is implemented, let's add some progression to our game. We will need to add levels. Each level should have one more enemy ship, and we can upgrade the damage and hit points of our ship in between the levels.

Adding a World class

We need to keep some values, such as the current level, in a separate entity, which we will describe as a `World` class.

Time for action – adding a World class

To implement our `World` class, we need to use the following steps:

1. Add a new Objective-C class called `World`, which is derived from `NSObject`.

2. To add a `level` property from the `int` type, do the following:

   ❑ Add a static variable called `level` in `World.h`, as shown in the following line of code:

   ```
   static int level;
   ```

   ❑ Add a static getter with the same name that returns the static variable, as shown in the following line of code:

   ```
   +(int) level;
   ```

   ❑ Add a static setter (`setLevel`) that sets the static variable, as shown in the following line of code:

   ```
   +(void) setLevel:(int)value;
   ```

3. Repeat step 2 for the properties `gold`, `hitpoints`, and `damage`.

4. We also need a `levelMax` property, but this one does not have a setter.

5. We need to import the `Assets.h` file inside the `World.m` file.

6. Add a static `reset` method that needs to be declared in `World.h`. It should look like the following piece of code:

   ```
   +(void) reset
   {
       level = 1;
       levelMax = 3;
       gold = 200;
       damage = [(NSNumber *) [Assets
         dictionaryFromJSON:@"gameplay.json"][@"damage"] intValue];
   ```

```
    hitpoints = [(NSNumber *) [Assets
    dictionaryFromJSON:@"gameplay.json"] [@"hitpoints"]
      intValue];
}
```

7. We also need a `log` method. It needs to be declared in `World.h` and needs to look like the following code:

```
+(void) log
{
    NSLog(@"Level %d of %d", level, levelMax);
    NSLog(@"Gold: %d", gold);
    NSLog(@"Players' hit points: %d", hitpoints);
    NSLog(@"Players' damage: %d", damage);
}
```

8. In `Game.m`, we need to call the `World` methods inside its initializer, as shown in the following code:

```
[director addScene:battlefield];

[World reset];
[World log];

[director showScene:@"battlefield"];
```

9. Run the example to see the result. We should now see the following output in the console:

```
PirateGame[4639:907] Level 1 of 3
PirateGame[4639:907] Gold: 200
PirateGame[4639:907] Players' hit points: 100
PirateGame[4639:907] Players' damage: 25
```

What just happened?

First of all, we created the `World` class. Objective-C does not support static properties. We can imitate that behavior of having a static property if we add static methods that have `methodName` as their name where we return a value. We also need to define a method called `setMethodName` that has a parameter. Now we can access `methodName` just like a property. However, inside the pseudo-getter, we can only access static variables.

After we were done with the setup, we needed to import the `Assets` class in step 5. After that, we added a `reset` method, which loaded the damage and hit points from our `gameplay.json` file. We set the `gold`, `level`, and `levelMax` variables to default values. In our case, the current level was the first one; we had a maximum of three levels, and 200 was the amount we had at our disposal at the start for the `gold` variable.

The `log` method that we implemented later logged all values except for the `levelMax` value. In step 8, we called the `reset` method, and we called `log` directly after that. When we ran the example, we saw the log output in the console.

Have a go hero

Right now, the `gold`, `level`, and `levelMax` variables are being set directly in the code. It's a better idea to load them from the `gameplay.json` file.

Updating the scene and dialog classes

Before we move on to implementing the progression system, there are a few small things we need to refactor. Let's tackle these issues:

◆ We have no way of resetting a scene if it's being shown again

◆ Multiline strings in dialogs are not displayed correctly

◆ We cannot access the dialog's buttons outside the `Dialog` class

◆ The dialog doesn't close after clicking on the buttons

Time for action – updating the scene and dialog classes

To add our first buttons, use the following steps:

1. Open the `Dialog.h` file.

2. Add properties for both **Yes** and **No** buttons using the following code:

```
@propertySPButton *buttonYes;
@propertySPButton *buttonNo;
```

3. Switch to `Dialog.m`.

4. Refactor all references from the local variables to use the properties.

5. Update the positions of `_title` and `_content` using the following code:

```
content = [SPTextField textFieldWithWidth:background.width -
    96.0f height:background.height - 150.0f text:@"Dialog default
    text"];
_content.x = 52.0f;
_content.y = 66.0f;

[SPTextField registerBitmapFontFromFile:@"PirateFont.fnt"];

_title = [SPTextField textFieldWithWidth:background.width * 0.6
    height:30.0f text:@"Dialog"];
```

```
_title.fontName = @"PirateFont";
_title.color = SP_WHITE;

_title.x = 36.0f;
_title.y = 26.0f;
```

6. In both onButtonYes and onButtonNo, add self.visible = NO; as the first statement.

7. In Scene.h, declare a method called reset using the following line of code:

   ```
   -(void) reset;
   ```

8. In Scene.m, implement the reset method with an empty body.

9. In SceneDirector.m, update this portion of code in the showScene method:

   ```
   if (_dict[name] != nil) {
     ((Scene *) _dict[name]).visible = YES;
     [((Scene *) _dict[name]) reset];

   }
   ```

10. Run the example.

    If we were to implement the reset method to the battlefield scene and add a logger message to the reset method of the battlefield scene, our output would change to this:

    ```
    PirateGame[4800:907] Level 1 of 3
    PirateGame[4800:907] Gold: 200
    PirateGame[4800:907] Players' hit points: 100
    PirateGame[4800:907] Players' damage: 25
    PirateGame[4800:907] Reset called.
    ```

What just happened?

We tackled the dialog issues first. In steps 2 to 4, we moved the buttons to be properties and updated all references inside the Dialog implementation. We then updated the position of the title and the message content. Long strings were not wider than the bounds of the dialog. In step 6, we hid the dialog once we tapped on any button.

For a scene to be able to reset itself, we first needed to add the reset method and just implement it as an empty method in Scene.m. We then needed to update the scene director to call the reset method from the current scene just after the scene turned visible.

If we ran the example now, and if we implemented the reset method in the battlefield scene and added a logger message, we would see that the reset method from the battlefield scene would actually be called.

Adding game mechanics to the pirate cove

Now that we have a `World` class and we have updated the `Dialog` and `Scene` classes to fit our needs, we can add some game mechanics to the pirate cove. The pirate cove is the place where we can upgrade our ship.

Time for action – making the pirate cove playable

To add game mechanics to the pirate cove, use the following steps:

1. Move the line of code `[SPTextField registerBitmapFontFromFile:@"PirateFont.fnt"];` from `Dialog.m` to the beginning of the `Game.m` file.

2. Add a button in `PirateCove.m`, as shown in the following code:

```
SPButton *buttonBattle = [SPButton buttonWithUpState:[[Assets
    textureAtlas:@"ui.xml"] textureByName:@"dialog_yes"];
text:@"Begin battle"];

buttonBattle.y = Sparrow.stage.height - buttonBattle.height -
    8.0f;
buttonBattle.x = (Sparrow.stage.width - buttonBattle.width) /
    2;

[buttonBattle addEventListenerForType:SP_EVENT_TYPE_TRIGGERED
    block:^(SPEvent *event){
    [((SceneDirector *) self.director) showScene:@"battlefield"];
}];
```

3. Add the button to the display tree using the following line of code:

```
[self addChild:buttonBattle];
```

4. In the following code, we add a text field to display the current amount of gold, which needs to be declared as an instance variable first:

```
_goldTextField =
    [SPTextField textFieldWithWidth:Sparrow.stage.width - 16.0f
        height:30.0f text:@"Gold"];
_goldTextField.fontName = @"PirateFont";
_goldTextField.color = SP_WHITE;

_goldTextField.x = 8.0f;
_goldTextField.y = 8.0f;
```

5. Add the text field to the display tree using the following line of code:

```
[self addChild:_goldTextField];
```

6. Add a method that updates the amount of gold on the screen using the following code:

```
-(void) updateGoldTextField
{
    _goldTextField.text = [NSString stringWithFormat:@"Gold:
  %d", World.gold];
}
```

7. Inside the `PirateCove.h` file, add an instance variable called `_dialogUpdateDamage` using the following line of code:

```
Dialog *_dialogUpdateDamage;
```

8. Add an instance variable called `_goldDamage` as shown in the following line of code:

```
int _goldDamage;
```

9. Inside the initializer, add the following piece of code for the first dialog:

```
_dialogUpdateDamage = [[Dialog alloc] init];

_dialogUpdateDamage.title.text = @"Update damage?";

_dialogUpdateDamage.x = (Sparrow.stage.width -
  _dialogUpdateDamage.width) / 2;
_dialogUpdateDamage.y = (Sparrow.stage.height -
  _dialogUpdateDamage.height) / 2;

_dialogUpdateDamage.visible = NO;

[weaponsmith addEventListenerForType:SP_EVENT_TYPE_TOUCH
  block:^(SPEvent *event){
  if (World.gold < _goldDamage) {
    _dialogUpdateDamage.buttonYes.enabled = NO;
  }

  _dialogUpdateDamage.visible = YES;
}];

[_dialogUpdateDamage addEventListener:@selector(onUpdateDamage:)
  atObject:self forType:EVENT_TYPE_YES_TRIGGERED];
```

10. Add the dialog to the display tree using the following line of code:

```
[self addChild:_dialogUpdateDamage];
```

11. Add the method `onUpdateDamage` as follows:

```
-(void) onUpdateDamage: (SPEvent *) event
{
World.damage = World.damage + (int) (World.damage / 10);
World.gold = World.gold - _goldDamage;
    [self updateGoldTextField];
}
```

12. Repeat steps 7 to 11 for the dialog that upgrades the hit points.

13. Add a `reset` method to the pirate cove scene as follows:

```
-(void) reset
{
    _goldDamage = (150 + (50 * (World.level - 1)));
    _dialogUpdateDamage.content.text =
      [NSString stringWithFormat:@"Increasing damage costs %d
        gold. Do you wish to proceed?", _goldDamage];

    _goldHitpoints = (200 + (75 * (World.level - 1)));
    _dialogUpdateHitpoints.content.text =
      [NSString stringWithFormat:@"Increasing hitpoints costs %d
        gold. Do you wish to proceed?", _goldHitpoints];

    [self updateGoldTextField];
}
```

14. Update the statement in the `Game.m` file to show the pirate cove when starting the game.

15. Run the example to see the result. We can now upgrade our ship in the pirate cove, as shown in the following screenshot:

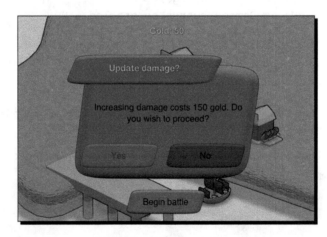

What just happened?

In step 1, we moved the registration of the bitmap font to the Game class. We only needed it once. Since we only had one dialog previously, it didn't really matter where we registered the font. However, as we now have multiple dialogs, the initializer of the dialog would register the font multiple times.

In step 2, we added a button that will be able to switch to the battlefield scene when we tap it. After we added the button to the display tree, we also added a text field to display the current amount of gold. We subsequently added the text field to the display tree. We also added a method that updates the text field.

In steps 6 to 11, we added a dialog to the screen that pops up when we tap the weaponsmith. It checks if we have enough gold at our disposal and lets us upgrade our damage if we do.

In step 13, we implemented the reset method. The intention is to make upgrading the ship more and more expensive depending on the current level.

Adding progression to the game

Everything is set in place for adding progression to the game.

Have a go hero –turning our game into a real game

Let's go ahead and implement game progression. The following are a few things you should keep in mind:

- The World values need to be reset before the battlefield instance is created
- Update the amount of gold once the player gets to a higher level
- Use the reset method of the battlefield scene to reset position and hit points
- There needs to be a way to keep track of all the sunken ships
- The enemies should probably be array-like objects
- The game itself should not start when the battlefield is initialized

After considering the preceding points, the game should look like what is shown in the following screenshot:

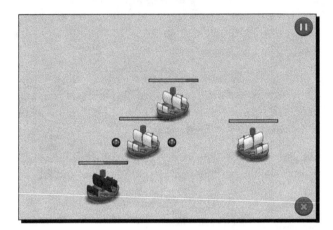

Take a look at how the preceding points can be implemented, and take these source files as the base for the following exercises:

- `Battlefield.h`: https://raw.github.com/freezedev/pirategame/9d5f53b5cb5e2e9bad822f0abd944e539e9bbf58/Classes/Battlefield.h
- `Battlefield.m`: https://raw.github.com/freezedev/pirategame/9d5f53b5cb5e2e9bad822f0abd944e539e9bbf58/Classes/Battlefield.m
- `Game.m`: https://raw.github.com/freezedev/pirategame/9d5f53b5cb5e2e9bad822f0abd944e539e9bbf58/Classes/Game.m
- `Ship.h`: https://raw.github.com/freezedev/pirategame/9d5f53b5cb5e2e9bad822f0abd944e539e9bbf58/Classes/Ship.h
- `Ship.m`: https://raw.github.com/freezedev/pirategame/9d5f53b5cb5e2e9bad822f0abd944e539e9bbf58/Classes/Ship.m
- `gameplay.json`: https://raw.github.com/freezedev/pirategame/9d5f53b5cb5e2e9bad822f0abd944e539e9bbf58/gameplay.json

Adding win and lose conditions

The last thing we will do in this chapter is add win and lose conditions for our game. Right now, we will just show a text field that displays whether we have won or lost.

Time for action – being able to win or lose

To be able to win or lose the game, use the following steps:

1. In `Ship.h`, add a callback property using the following line of code:

```
@property (nonatomic, copy) ShipCallbackonDead;
```

2. This callback property gets invoked if the ship is equal to or less than zero hit points, as shown in the following code:

```
if (_hitpoints<= 0) {
  self.visible = FALSE;

  if (self.onDead) {
    [_onDead invoke];
  }
}
```

3. In the `Battlefield.h` file, add two properties for our new text fields as shown:

```
@property SPTextField *textGameWon;
@property SPTextField *textGameLost;
```

4. In the initializer, add the following piece of code:

```
_textGameLost =
  [SPTextField textFieldWithWidth:Sparrow.stage.width height:
    Sparrow.stage.height text:@"Game Over"];
_textGameLost.fontName = @"PirateFont";
_textGameLost.color = SP_WHITE;
_textGameLost.visible = NO;

_textGameWon =
  [SPTextField textFieldWithWidth:Sparrow.stage.width height:
    Sparrow.stage.height text:@"You won the game. Well done"];
_textGameWon.fontName = @"PirateFont";
_textGameWon.color = SP_WHITE;
_textGameWon.visible = NO;

__weak typeof(self) weakSelf = self;
_pirateShip.onDead = ^{
  weakSelf.textGameLost.visible = YES;
};
//...
[self addChild:_textGameLost];
[self addChild:_textGameWon];
```

5. Inside the `onEnterFrame` method, update the progression system by adding the winning condition as shown:

```
if (deadCount == World.level) {
  if (World.level == World.levelMax) {
    self.textGameWon.visible = YES;
  } else {
    World.gold = World.gold + (250 * World.level);
    World.level++;
    self.paused = YES;
    [((SceneDirector *) self.director)
      showScene:@"piratecove"];
  }
}
```

6. Run the example to see the result.

If we now win or lose the game, a text field will be displayed on the screen, as shown in the following screenshot:

What just happened?

We needed to know the exact point when a ship gets destroyed, so we added a callback in steps 1 and 2. Precisely at the moment when the player ship gets destroyed, we wanted to display something to inform that the player has lost the game.

We then added the text fields in steps 3 and 4. The only thing we needed to consider here is that we need to access `self` (the instance itself) inside the block. Typically, we can't access any property from `self` in the block, but we do need this because the text field is a property on the instance itself. So, we needed to use an unsafe reference by using the `__weak` keyword. This is something that should be used with caution and, in general, only as a last resort. We also needed to make sure that the text fields were added as the last elements to the display tree so that they were always on top of all other elements. After we added the lose condition, we added the win condition in step 5. When we ran the example, we saw a text popping up if we either lost or won the game.

Technically, we could also have created the text field dynamically once we won. It is best practice, however, to create everything at the beginning, especially with complex projects.

Pop quiz

Q1. `SPPoint` provides a method to get the distance between two points.

1. True
2. False

Q2. A finite state machine always needs transitions.

1. True
2. False

Q3. If we want to modify a local variable inside a block, what do we need to do?

1. Make it a weak reference
2. Prefix the variable with `__block`
3. Refactor it to a property

Summary

In this chapter, we learned about artificial intelligence. Specifically, we covered fuzzy logic and finite state machines, and we also added more gameplay elements.

Now that our game is feature-complete but rough around the edges, let's add some audio to our game—which is the topic of the next chapter.

9
Adding Audio to Our Game

In the previous chapter, we learned about artificial intelligence. We learned theory about finite state machines and fuzzy logic. We applied these elements to our game. We also implemented the remaining gameplay elements into our game. In this chapter, we are going to add music and sound to our game. Audio in itself is an important aspect to any game as it is part of the player's experience. Try to play your favorite game without music and you'll find yourself having a different experience when playing the game.

We will cover the following topics in this chapter:

◆ Loading sound and music files

◆ Generating our own sound effects

◆ Playing audio

Let's add music and sound to our game, shall we?

Finding music and sound

When developing a game, the developer is usually not a jack of all trades and may have a hard time when looking for sound and music. Apple's own GarageBand provides an easy way to create music using predefined loops or even one's own instruments. Another possibility is to find talented people who can help to create audio files. One of the places to look out for are the TIGSource forums—a place for independent game developers—which has a portfolio section at `http://forums.tigsource.com/index.php?board=43.0` and a section that offers paid work at `http://forums.tigsource.com/index.php?board=40.0`.

Generating sound effects

Bxfr is a procedural sound generator which is often used in game jams. It is available online at `http://www.bfxr.net/`; the standalone versions for Windows and Mac OS X can be downloaded from this link as well. Its purpose is to generate 8-bit sound effects in just a few clicks:

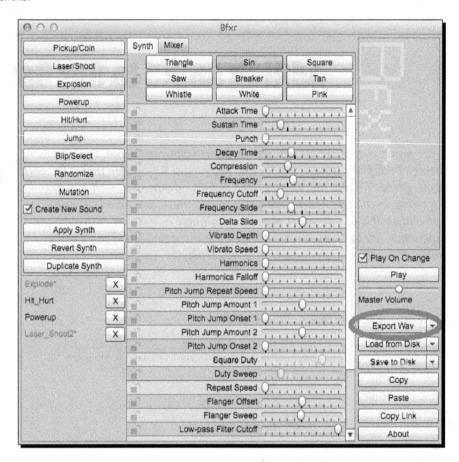

First of all, we need to select a type, which we can then modify with several sliders such as the frequency or the length of the sound.

Once we are done, we can export the sound effect using the **Export Wav** button.

Learning about audio formats

Sparrow allows all audio files supported by iOS to be loaded. Some audio codecs support hardware-assisted decoding, while others don't.

The iOS devices contain specialized hardware that can handle the encoding and decoding of certain audio formats (for example, AIFC), thereby freeing up the CPU that would otherwise be required to handle these expensive operations. The drawback of the hardware-assisted approach is that only one file can be handled at a time. For example, you can't play background music and sound effects with it simultaneously.

For more information about how iOS handles audio playback, take a look at Apple's documentation at `https://developer.apple.com/library/ios/documentation/audiovideo/conceptual/multimediapg/UsingAudio/UsingAudio.html`.

The best formats for audio formats in Sparrow are AIFC and CAFF.

Let's see what they are:

♦ AIFC is a compressed **Audio Interchange Format** (**AIFF**) file. This is usually the best option for background music. There is one other thing to consider: if the audio playback is hardware-assisted (as it is in the case of AIFC), only one file can be played at a time.

♦ The **Core Audio File Format** (**CAFF**) is an uncompressed audio format. This format is best used for short sound effects.

Both these formats have the lowest footprint on the CPU. If application size is an issue, there is an unconventional way to solve this: some devices still only have mono speakers, so converting audio files to mono could be a valid option if there are a lot of sound files.

To convert audio files, the iOS SDK provides a command-line tool called **afconvert**. Assuming our audio file is called `myAudioFile.wav`, we can use the following examples:

♦ **Convert to CAFF**: The command to convert to CAFF is `afconvert -f caff -d LE16 myAudioFile.wav`

♦ **Convert to AIFC**: The command to convert to AIFC is `afconvert -f AIFC -d ima4 myAudioFile.wav`

Music and sound effects for our game

The necessary audio files are once again uploaded to our GitHub repository. In order to use them, download them from `https://github.com/freezedev/pirategame-assets/releases/download/0.9/Audio_09.zip`, extract the file, and copy the contents in our template. When copying the files to the project, we need to make sure that we add them to the target.

Adding audio playback

Now that we know about audio formats, we can generate sounds for ourselves if needed, and if we have the necessary files, we can play some audio.

Starting the audio engine

Before we can play any sounds, we need to start the audio engine.

Time for action – getting audio files to play

Perform the following steps to start the audio engine:

1. Open our Xcode project if it's not already open.

2. Switch to the Game.m file.

3. Inside the initializer, start the audio engine as shown; it should be one of the first few statements:

   ```
   [SPAudioEngine start];
   ```

4. Add a dealloc method that stops the audio engine:

   ```
   -(void) dealloc
   {
       [SPAudioEngine stop];
   }
   ```

5. Run the example.

When we run this example in the simulator, we might see the following lines in the console:

```
AudioStreamBasicDescription:  2 ch,  44100 Hz, 'lpcm' (0x00000029) 32-bit
little-endian float, deinterleaved
```

What just happened?

To play any audio file, we need to start the audio engine at the start of our application, which in our case, is the initializer from the Game class.

There are different operational modes for the audio engine, which influence how the iPod music app will behave when we run our game.

If the audio is muted, the game audio will be muted as well. This is the default operational mode; other modes include the game audio continue even when the device is muted or the iPod music mixes with the game audio. Take a look at what the latter will look like in code:

```
[SPAudioEngine start: SPAudioSessionCategory_AmbientSound];
```

For more through information, take a look at the Sparrow SPAudioEngine documentation at `http://doc.sparrow-framework.org/v2/Classes/SPAudioEngine.html`.

When we run this example, we get some information about the audio engine in the console.

Have a go hero

Currently, the audio engine starts and stops when the game starts or stops, respectively. It's also a good idea to start and stop the engine if the background and foreground events (such as `applicationWillResignActive` and `applicationDidBecomeActive`) are triggered.

Playing music in our scenes

Now that the audio engine is up and running, let's play the background music.

Time for action – playing music in our scenes

Perform the following steps to play background music in our scenes:

1. Open the `Scene.h` file.

2. Add an instance variable named `backgroundMusic`, which is a pointer to `SPSoundChannel` using the following line of code:

   ```
   SPSoundChannel *backgroundMusic;
   ```

3. Declare a method called `stop` as follows:

   ```
   -(void) stop;
   ```

4. Inside the `Scene.m` file, define the `stop` method with an empty body.

5. Update the `showScene` method in the `SceneDirector.m` file to fit the following block of code:

   ```
   -(void) showScene:(NSString *)name
   {
       for (NSString* sceneName in _dict) {
           ((Scene *) _dict[sceneName]).visible = NO;
           [((Scene *) _dict[sceneName]) stop];
       }
   ```

```
        if (_dict[name] != nil) {
            ((Scene *) _dict[name]).visible = YES;
            [((Scene *) _dict[name]) reset];


        }
    }
```

6. Switch to `PirateCove.m`.

7. Inside the initializer, add the following lines at the top:

```
SPSound *sound = [Assets sound:@"music_cove.aifc"];
backgroundMusic = [sound createChannel];
backgroundMusic.loop = YES;
```

8. Update the `reset` method to look like the following:

```
-(void) reset
{
    [backgroundMusic play];

    _goldDamage = (150 + (50 * (World.level - 1)));
    _dialogUpdateDamage.content.text = [NSString
      stringWithFormat:@"Increasing damage costs %d gold. Do
        you wish to proceed?", _goldDamage];

    _goldHitpoints = (200 + (75 * (World.level - 1)));
    _dialogUpdateHitpoints.content.text = [NSString
      stringWithFormat:@"Increasing hitpoints costs %d gold. Do
        you wish to proceed?", _goldHitpoints];

    [self updateGoldTextField];
}
```

9. Implement the scene's `stop` method as follows:

```
-(void) stop
{
    [backgroundMusic stop];
}
```

10. Run the example and you will see the following output. We can now hear the music in the background.

What just happened?

First of all, we added an instance variable (`backgroundMusic`) to hold the background music. The `SPSound` variable holds the data of a sound file while `SPSoundChannel` plays the sound itself, similar to the relationship between `SPTexture` and `SPImage`. It is recommended that you keep a reference to `SPSoundChannel`. This is required if we want to stop the playback sound for any reason whatsoever.

To allow us to have background music in multiple scenes, we need to stop the background music from the current scene and start the music from the next scene because we don't want to run into any nasty side effects. These side effects are that the first music file will use the hardware codec and the second one will use software decoding, thereby heavily impacting the performance of our game. Both music files will play, though.

If we want to stop the background music when we are in the scene, we can utilize the scene's `reset` method. Now, we wanted to do the same only when the scene is deactivated. We first declared the `stop` method for exactly this purpose in step 3 and implemented it as an empty method in the step afterwards. In the `SceneManager` class, we need to call the `stop` method of each scene when we are hiding the scene.

Inside the initializer of the `PirateCove` scene, we created a local `SPSound` variable that loads the music file through our asset management system. We then used the `createChannel` method and saved the result in the instance variable. We want to loop the music endlessly, so we set the `loop` property to `YES`.

In step 8, we updated the `reset` method to play the background music and in step 9, we overwrote the `stop` method and stopped the background music.

When we run this example now, we can hear the music playing in a loop.

Have a go hero

Now that the pirate cove scene has some background music, go ahead and give the battlefield some music.

Adding a sound effect

Our audio engine is up and running; we already know that it works because we have played some music, and now it's time to add the sound effects.

Time for action – sound effects in the pirate cove

To add sound effects to the pirate cove scene, perform the following steps:

1. Open the `PirateCove.m` file.

2. Update both the `onUpdateDamage` and `onUpdateHitpoints` methods to play a sound effect, as shown in the following code:

```
-(void) onUpdateDamage: (SPEvent *) event
{
    World.damage = World.damage + (int) (World.damage / 10);
    World.gold = World.gold - _goldDamage;
    [self updateGoldTextField];

    [[Assets sound:@"powerup.caf"] play];
}

-(void) onUpdateHitpoints: (SPEvent *) event
{
    World.hitpoints = World.hitpoints + (int) (World.hitpoints
      / 5);
    World.gold = World.gold - _goldHitpoints;
    [self updateGoldTextField];

    [[Assets sound:@"powerup.caf"] play];
}
```

3. Run the example and you will see the following output. We can now hear a sound if we successfully upgrade our pirate ship.

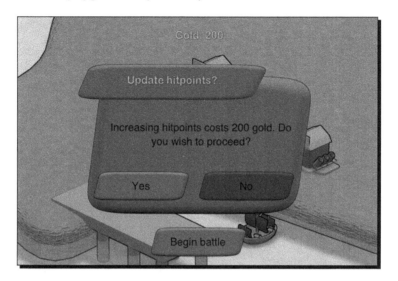

What just happened?

Inside the pirate cove scene, we added a sound effect to both the onUpdateDamage and the onUpdateHitpoints methods. We got the powerup file through the asset management system and then played the sound directly. This method is useful for short sounds and at places where we don't need to keep a reference to manipulate the playback of the audio channel afterwards.

Now, when we run this example, we can hear a sound effect once we successfully upgrade our ship.

Have a go hero

Go ahead and add the following sound effects in the battlefield:

- When a ship is hit (the hit method in the Ship class)
- When a ship shoots (the shoot method in the Ship class)
- When a ship gets destroyed (hit points getter in the Ship class)

Pop quiz

Q1. AAC audio files offer hardware-assisted encoding.

1. True
2. False

Q2. If SPSound only contains the sound data, which class should be used to play an audio file?

1. AVAudioSession
2. SPSoundChannel
3. SPAudio

Q3. To play any sounds at all, we need to initialize the audio engine.

1. True
2. False

Summary

In this chapter, we learned how to load and play audio files. Specifically, we covered data formats and the basic usage of audio in Sparrow.

Now that our game has some audio, let's polish our game—which is the topic of the next chapter.

10
Polishing Our Game

In the previous chapter, we added sound and music to our game. We also learned about audio file formats and even how to generate our own sound effects.

In this chapter, we are going to polish our game. We will be covering the following topics in this chapter:

- ◆ Improving the game over mechanism
- ◆ Adding a minimalistic tutorial
- ◆ Loading and saving the current state of the game

Polishing is the process of giving the last finishing touches to the game. There is a saying in software development that the last 20 percent of the development feels as hard as the first 80 percent. With such motivation, let's polish our game, shall we?

Adding additional scenes

Our game still feels rough around the edges. Our first order of business is to add more scenes, which should make the game feel more rounded, especially when starting the game and when the game is over.

The game over scene

Currently, the game over mechanism is a bit too minimalistic. While the player can lose and win the game, they can't restart the game once it is over. The player needs to shut down the application and open it again.

This is counterintuitive as the default behavior of iOS apps is to freeze the app instead of shutting it down. So in the worst case, our game with the **Game Over** message stays in the memory until the device is rebooted or the user kills the application from the app switcher.

Creating the game over scene

As our first task, we are going to decouple the game over logic and move it into a separate scene. Our game over scene should show whether the game was won or lost.

Time for action – showing the game over scene

Use the following steps to create the game over scene:

1. Open our Xcode project if it's not already open.

2. Create a new Objective-C class inside the `GameScenes` group.

3. Call this class `GameOver` it should be a subclass of `Scene`.

4. Switch to the `GameOver.h` file.

5. Using the following line of code, add a property called `message`:

   ```
   @property SPTextField *message;
   ```

6. Using the following line of code, add another property to indicate whether the game was won:

   ```
   @property (nonatomic) BOOL gameWon;
   ```

7. Switch to `GameOver.m`.

8. Import the `SceneDirector.h`, `Assets.h`, and the `World.h` files, as shown in the following code:

   ```
   #import "SceneDirector.h"
   #import "Assets.h"
   #import "World.h"
   ```

9. Add an initializer for this new scene, as shown in the following code:

   ```
   -(id) init
   {
       if ((self = [super init])) {

           SPImage *background = [SPImage imageWithTexture:[Assets
               texture:@"water.png"]];

           _message = [SPTextField
               textFieldWithWidth:Sparrow.stage.width
                   height:Sparrow.stage.height text:@"Game Over"
   ```

```
                fontName:@"PirateFont" fontSize:24.0f
                   color:SP_WHITE];

            SPTexture *yesButton = [[Assets textureAtlas:@"ui.xml"]
               textureByName:@"dialog_yes"];
        SPButton *resetButton = [SPButton buttonWithUpState:yesButton
          text:@"Start over"];

            resetButton.x = (Sparrow.stage.width -
               resetButton.width) / 2;
            resetButton.y = Sparrow.stage.height -
               resetButton.height - 8.0f;

            [resetButton
               addEventListenerForType:SP_EVENT_TYPE_TRIGGERED
                 block:^(id event) {
                 [World reset];
                 [(SceneDirector *) self.director
                    showScene:@"piratecove"];
            }];

            [self addChild:background];
            [self addChild:_message];
            [self addChild:resetButton];
        }

        return self;
    }
```

10. Add a getter for the gameWon property, as shown in the following code:

```
-(BOOL) getGameWon
{
    return _gameWon;
}
```

11. Now, add the setter for the gameWon property, as shown in the following code:

```
-(void) setGameWon:(BOOL)gameWon
{
    _gameWon = gameWon;

    if (_gameWon) {
        _message.text = @"You won the game. Congratulations.";
    } else {
        _message.text = @"Your ship sank. Try again.";
    }
}
```

12. Switch to `Game.m`.

13. Import the `GameOver.h` file using the following line of code:

```
#import "GameOver.h"
```

14. Then, create an instance of the `GameOver` scene using the following code:

```
GameOver *gameOver = [[GameOver alloc]
    initWithName:@"gameover"];
```

15. Add the game over instance to the scene director using the following code:

```
[director addScene:gameOver];
```

16. Show the game over scene by default using the following line of code:

```
[director showScene:@"gameover"];
```

17. Run the example and we will see the game over scene, as shown in the following screenshot:

What just happened?

As we have done before, we opened our Xcode project. Then, we created a class, which is going to be our game over scene. It's called `GameOver` and is a subclass of `Scene`.

In the `GameOver` header file, we added two properties in step 5 and 6, respectively. The first property is the message that will be displayed on the screen. The second is to indicate whether the game was won. We added a custom getter and setter for this property later on. We marked this property as non-atomic, as we don't really need thread safety and we used only one thread anyway.

In the `GameOver.m` file, we imported all the necessary headers, which are as follows:

- The asset manager from `Assets.h`, as it is most likely that we load an asset
- The scene director from `SceneDirector.h`, because we need to switch to another scene
- The `World` class from `World.h`, as we need to reset our in-game values

Then, we added the initializer. Our game over scene consists of the following:

- Water as the background
- The text field which is the `message` property
- The reset button

In this example, we used the `SPTextField` factory method (also known as a convenience constructor) that lets us define the width, height, text, font name, font size, and color in a single step. One thing we need to consider is to keep the font size similar to the original bitmap font size. If it's much bigger than the original size, the font gets all pixelated and washed out.

There is a way to get around this though: if we set `SP_NATIVE_FONT_SIZE` as the font size for the font instance, it will automatically calculate its actual size so that it is displayed as sharp as possible.

We defined the touch event for the reset button as a block and reset all of our in-game values and switched to the pirate cove scene. After this, we added all of our display objects to the display tree.

Then, we defined our custom getter and setter for our `gameWon` property:

- **Getter**: This simply returns the internal _gameWon value
- **Setter**: After we set the property value, we updated the message depending on its value

In the `Game` class, we need to create an instance of the `GameOver` scene, which we then added to the scene director. In step 16, we updated the default scene to be the game over scene.

When we ran the example in the last step, we saw the game over scene.

Connecting the game over scene

Now that we have our game over scene, let's integrate it into the game.

Time for action – having the game over scene show up

To incorporate the game over scene into the game, use the following steps:

1. Switch to the `Battlefield.h` file.
2. Remove both the `textGameWon` and `textGameLost` properties.
3. Switch to the `Battlefield.m` file.
4. Remove all references to the `textGameWon` and `textGameLost` properties.

5. In the `GameOver.m` file, add a `reset` method using the following code:

```
-(void) reset
{
    self.gameWon = NO;
}
```

6. In the `SceneDirector.h` file, add a property called `currentScene` using the following code:

```
@property (readonly) Scene *currentScene;
```

7. In the `SceneDirector.m` file, update the `showScene` method to set the `currentScene` property, as shown in the following code:

```
-(void) showScene:(NSString *)name
{
    for (NSString* sceneName in _dict) {
        ((Scene *) _dict[sceneName]).visible = false;
        [((Scene *) _dict[sceneName]) stop];
    }

    if (_dict[name] != nil) {
        ((Scene *) _dict[name]).visible = YES;
        [((Scene *) _dict[name]) reset];
        _currentScene = (Scene *) _dict[name];
    }
}
```

8. Switch to the `Battlefield.m` file.

9. Update the `reset` method to set the visibility of the ships, as shown in the following code:

```
-(void) reset
{
    self.paused = NO;

    _pirateShip.x = [(NSNumber *) [Assets
      dictionaryFromJSON:@"gameplay.json"][@"battlefield"]
        [@"pirate"][@"x"] floatValue];
    _pirateShip.y = [(NSNumber *) [Assets
      dictionaryFromJSON:@"gameplay.json"][@"battlefield"]
        [@"pirate"][@"y"] floatValue];

    [_pirateShip reset];
    _pirateShip.visible = YES;

    for (int i = 0; i < [_enemyShip count]; i++) {
```

```
    ((Ship *) _enemyShip[i]).x = [(NSNumber *) [Assets
      dictionaryFromJSON:@"gameplay.json"][@"battlefield"]
        [@"enemy"][i][@"x"] floatValue];
    ((Ship *) _enemyShip[i]).y = [(NSNumber *) [Assets
      dictionaryFromJSON:@"gameplay.json"][@"battlefield"]
        [@"enemy"][i][@"y"] floatValue];
    [((Ship *) _enemyShip[i]) reset];
    ((Ship *) _enemyShip[i]).visible = NO;
    }


    for (int i = 0; i < World.level; i++) {
        ((Ship *) _enemyShip[i]).visible = YES;
        [self updateAI:_enemyShip[i] withState:_aiState];
    }
}
```

10. Update the condition to win the game, as shown in the following code:

```
if (deadCount == World.level) {
  if (World.level == World.levelMax) {
    [(SceneDirector *) self.director showScene:@"gameover"];
    ((GameOver *) ((SceneDirector *)
      self.director).currentScene).gameWon = YES;
  } else {
    World.gold = World.gold + (250 * World.level);
    World.level++;
    self.paused = YES;
    [((SceneDirector *) self.director)
      showScene:@"piratecove"];
  }
}
```

11. Next, update the condition to lose the game, as shown in the following code:

```
__weak typeof(self) weakSelf = self;
_pirateShip.onDead = ^{
  [(SceneDirector *) weakSelf.director showScene:@"gameover"];
  ((GameOver *) ((SceneDirector *)
    weakSelf.director).currentScene).gameWon = NO;
};
```

12. In Game.m, change the default scene back to the pirate cove.

13. Run the example. When we run the example and once we actually lose the game, we see the following screen:

What just happened?

In the `Battlefield` header file, we removed the text field properties that show up when the game was won or lost. Then, we removed all code portions that reference these properties in `Battlefield.m`.

In step 5, we added a `reset` method for our `GameOver` scene, where we set the `gameWon` property to `NO`. The difference between this scene switch is that we need to set the `gameWon` property after the scene has been switched. In order to facilitate this, we updated the scene director.

In the next step, we added a read-only property called `currentScene` that gives us a reference to the current scene. After this, we updated the `showScene` method to set the current scene. This happened right after we set the current scene to be visible and called the `reset` method.

In the battlefield scene, we first updated the visibilities of our ships. If we hadn't done this, the enemy ships would stay visible even after we reset the game.

In steps 10 and 11, we updated the win and lose conditions. We imported the `GameOver.h` file here as well, in order to cast the `currentScene` property to a pointer to the `GameOver` class.

The last thing we did was change back to the pirate cove scene. When we ran the example and when we lost or won the game, the game over scene was shown and we were able to restart the game.

Adding a main menu

Next, we are going to add a simple main menu.

Time for action – integrating the main menu into our game

Use the following steps to add a main menu:

1. Add a new class called `MainMenu` which should be a subclass of `Scene`.

2. Switch to `MainMenu.m`.

3. Import `Assets.h` and `SceneDirector.h`.

4. Add the initializer for the main menu, as shown in the following code:

```
-(id) init
{
    if ((self = [super init])) {

        SPImage *background = [SPImage imageWithTexture:[Assets
            texture:@"water.png"]];

    SPTexture *shipTexture = [[Assets
      textureAtlas:@"ship_pirate_small_cannon.xml"]
        textureByName:@"ne_0001"];
        SPImage *ship = [SPImage imageWithTexture:shipTexture];
        ship.x = 16.0f;
        ship.y = (Sparrow.stage.height - ship.height) / 2;

    SPTexture *dialogTexture = [[Assets textureAtlas:@"ui.xml"]
      textureByName:@"dialog_yes"];
        SPButton *buttonNewGame = [SPButton
          buttonWithUpState:dialogTexture text:@"New game"];

        buttonNewGame.x = (Sparrow.stage.width -
          buttonNewGame.width) / 2;
        buttonNewGame.y = 50.0f;

        [buttonNewGame
          addEventListenerForType:SP_EVENT_TYPE_TRIGGERED
            block:^(id event) {
            [(SceneDirector *) self.director
              showScene:@"piratecove"];
        }];

        SPButton *buttonContinue = [SPButton
          buttonWithUpState:dialogTexture text:@"Continue"];

        buttonContinue.x = (Sparrow.stage.width -
          buttonContinue.width) / 2;
        buttonContinue.y = 150.0f;
```

```
            buttonContinue.enabled = NO;

            [self addChild:background];
            [self addChild:ship];
            [self addChild:buttonNewGame];
            [self addChild:buttonContinue];
        }

        return self;
    }
```

5. Switch to Game.m.

6. Import MainMenu.h using the following line of code:

   ```
   #import "MainMenu.h"
   ```

7. Using the following code, create a local variable for the main menu that will hold an instance of the MainMenu class.

   ```
   MainMenu *mainMenu = [[MainMenu alloc]
       initWithName:@"mainmenu"];
   ```

8. Add the mainMenu instance to the director, as shown in the following code:

   ```
   [director addScene:mainMenu];
   ```

9. Update the showScene call to the main menu scene, as shown in the following code:

   ```
   [director showScene:@"mainmenu"];
   ```

10. Run the example and we will see the main menu, as shown in the following screenshot:

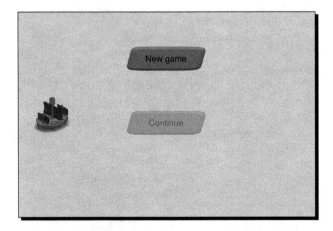

What just happened?

To add a main menu, we needed a class subclassed from `Scene`. Once the class was created, we imported the asset management system and the scene director.

In step 3, we added the initializer. Our main menu consists of the following:

- The same background that we used in the battlefield and other scenes
- A pirate ship
- A button to start a new game
- A button to continue the game

For the new game, we used a block for its touch event, which switches to the pirate cove scene. The **Continue** button does not have an event yet and is disabled. After this, we need to take all our elements to the display tree.

In steps 5 to 9, we added the main menu to our game class in a manner similar to how we added the game over scene.

When we ran the example, we saw the main menu.

Have a go hero

The main menu now only has two buttons. Typically, a main menu offers a bit more than this such as buttons to switch to the options menu or the credits screen. In some instances, the main menu even has buttons to navigate to social sites. Go ahead and add the options and credits screens, which can be opened from the main menu.

Adding an intro scene

An intro scene is a perfect way to introduce the player to the characters, the story or the art style of a game. An intro is not necessary for all games; in fact, it's best used if it fits into the overall game and style of the game.

As we don't have a story or characters, we are going to show two ships moving near each other, shooting each other, and eventually one of the ships sinks.

Time for action – creating an intro for our game

Use the following steps to add the intro scene:

1. This is as good a time as any to move the collision detection code into a separate file. Create a new group called `Logic` and add a class inside this group called `Collision` which is a subclass of `NSObject`.

2. Declare this static method in the `Collision` class, as shown in the following code:

```
+(void) checkShipCollision: (Ship *) ship1 againstShip: (Ship
  *) ship2 withReferenceToSprite: (SPSprite *) sprite;
```

3. Inside `Collision.m`, implement the `checkShipCollision` method with the following lines of code:

```
SPRectangle *enemyShipBounds = [ship1 boundsInSpace:sprite];
SPRectangle *ball1 = [ship2.cannonBallLeft
  boundsInSpace:sprite];
SPRectangle *ball2 = [ship2.cannonBallRight
  boundsInSpace:sprite];

if ([enemyShipBounds intersectsRectangle:ball1] ||
  [enemyShipBounds intersectsRectangle:ball2]) {
  if (ship2.cannonBallLeft.visible ||
    ship2.cannonBallRight.visible) {
    [ship2 abortShooting];
    if (ship1.type == ShipPirate) {
      [ship1 hit: World.damage];
    } else {
      [ship1 hit:[(NSNumber *) [Assets
        dictionaryFromJSON:@"gameplay.json"][@"damage"]
          intValue]];
    }
  }
}
```

4. In order for this code to work, we need to import `Assets.h` and `World.h` in the `Collision.m` file.

5. In `Battlefield.m`, delete the collision code, import `Collision.h`, and use the new method from the `Collision` class now:

```
for (int i = 0; i < World.level; i++) {
  [Collision checkShipCollision:_pirateShip
    againstShip:_enemyShip[i] withReferenceToSprite:self];
  [Collision checkShipCollision:_enemyShip[i]
    againstShip:_pirateShip withReferenceToSprite:self];

  [_enemyShip[i] advanceTime:passedTime];
  if (((Ship *) _enemyShip[i]).isDead) {
    deadCount++;
  }
}
```

6. Add the intro scene by subclassing `Scene` and call it `Intro`. This should be done inside the `GameScenes` group.

7. In `Intro.h`, import `Ship.h` and add two instance variables, one for the pirate ship and one for the enemy ship, as shown in the following code:

```
@interface Intro : Scene {
    Ship *_pirateShip;
    Ship *_enemyShip;
}
```

8. Switch to `Intro.m`.

9. Add an initializer for the `Intro` class with the help of the following code:

```
-(id) init
{
    if ((self = [super init])) {

        SPImage *background = [SPImage imageWithTexture:[Assets
          texture:@"water.png"]];

        _pirateShip = [[Ship alloc] initWithType:ShipPirate];
        _pirateShip.x = 16.0f;
        _pirateShip.y = ((Sparrow.stage.height -
          _pirateShip.height) / 2) - 20.0f;

        _enemyShip = [[Ship alloc] initWithType:ShipNormal];
        _enemyShip.x = Sparrow.stage.width - _enemyShip.width -
          16.0f;
        _enemyShip.y = ((Sparrow.stage.height -
          _enemyShip.height) / 2) + 20.0f;

        [self addEventListener:@selector(onEnterFrame:)
          atObject:self forType:SP_EVENT_TYPE_ENTER_FRAME];

        SPButton *buttonNext = [SPButton
          buttonWithUpState:[[Assets textureAtlas:@"ui.xml"]
            textureByName:@"dialog_yes"] text:@"Next"];

        buttonNext.x = (Sparrow.stage.width - buttonNext.width)
          / 2;
        buttonNext.y = Sparrow.stage.height - buttonNext.height
          - 8.0f;

        [buttonNext
          addEventListenerForType:SP_EVENT_TYPE_TRIGGERED
            block:^(id event) {
            [(SceneDirector *) self.director
              showScene:@"piratecove"];
        }];
```

```
        [self addChild:background];
        [self addChild:_pirateShip];
        [self addChild:_enemyShip];
        [self addChild:buttonNext];
    }

    return self;
}
```

10. Add the event listener for `onEnterFrame`, as shown in the following code:

```
-(void) onEnterFrame: (SPEnterFrameEvent *) event
{
    double passedTime = event.passedTime;

    [Collision checkShipCollision:_pirateShip
      againstShip:_enemyShip withReferenceToSprite:self];
    [Collision checkShipCollision:_enemyShip
      againstShip:_pirateShip withReferenceToSprite:self];

    [_pirateShip advanceTime:passedTime];
    [_enemyShip advanceTime:passedTime];
}
```

11. Add a reset method, as shown in the following code:

```
-(void) reset
{
    [_pirateShip reset];
    [_enemyShip reset];

    [_pirateShip moveToX:Sparrow.stage.width / 2
      andY:(Sparrow.stage.height / 2) - 20.0f withBlock:^{
        [_pirateShip.juggler delayInvocationByTime:1.5f
          block:^{
            [_pirateShip shootWithBlock:^{
                [_pirateShip shootWithBlock:^{
                    [_pirateShip shootWithBlock:^{
                        [_pirateShip.juggler
                          delayInvocationByTime:1.0f block:^{
                            [_pirateShip shoot];
                        }];
                    }];
                }];
            }];
        }];
    }];
```

```
}];

    [_enemyShip moveToX:Sparrow.stage.width / 2
      andY:(Sparrow.stage.height / 2) + 20.0f withBlock:^{
        [_enemyShip shoot];
      }];
}
```

12. In `MainMenu.m`, show the intro scene if the new game button has been touched.

13. In `Game.m`, import `Intro.h`, create an instance of the `Intro` class, and add it the director.

14. Run the example.

When we start a new game, we see the intro in action, as shown in the following code:

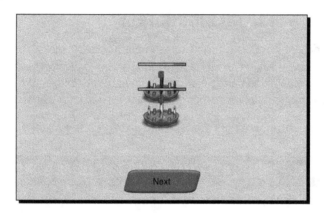

What just happened?

As we needed the collision detection in both the intro and the game itself, we moved it into its own class. When we moved the checkShipCollision method, we added an additional parameter. This parameter was then passed as a reference to the `boundsInSpace` method. We imported the asset management and the `World` class for this code snippet to work.

In the next step, we updated the collision in the battlefield scene.

We then added a new scene called `Intro`, where we first added two instance variables, one for our own ship and one for the pirate ship. In step 9, we added the initializer, which perform the following:

- Add the water background
- Initialize both ship instances
- Add a button to skip the intro

We then added an event listener to skip the event listener and switch to the pirate cove scene. We also added an event listener for the enter frame event. We then added all elements to the display tree

In step 10, we implemented the `onEnterFrame` event listener, which calls the collision method and advances the time of both ships.

The `reset` method calls the `reset` method of these ships and moves the ships to the center of the screen. The enemy ship can shoot only once, while the pirate ships can shoot multiple times to kill the enemy ship.

We showed the intro scene in the main menu. After this, we added the `Intro` class to the game class, and when we ran the example, we saw the intro scene when we started a new game.

Implementing tutorial mechanics

There are many different ways for tutorials to be implemented. It may range from just showing an image with controls, to having an interactive experience, to displaying a control scheme each time the player is about to perform an action. In general, the last two options could be achieved with a finite state machine, similar to the one we used for our artificial intelligence.

For our purposes, we will update the intro scene to display hints while the animation is playing.

Time for action – adding a tutorial to our intro scene

Follow these steps to display hints during the intro:

1. In `Intro.h`, add an instance variable called message:

   ```
   SPTextField *_message;
   ```

2. Switch to `Intro.m`.

3. Update the initializer with the help of the following code:

   ```
   [buttonNext addEventListenerForType:SP_EVENT_TYPE_TRIGGERED
     block:^(id event) {
     [(SceneDirector *) self.director showScene:@"piratecove"];
   }];

   SPQuad *quad = [SPQuad quadWithWidth:400.0f height:60.0f
     color:SP_BLACK];
   ```

```
quad.alpha = 0.8f;
quad.x = 16.0f;
quad.y = 16.0f;

_message = [SPTextField textFieldWithWidth:400.0f height:60.0f
    text:@"Welcome to the battlefield."];
_message.color = SP_WHITE;
_message.x = 16.0f;
_message.y = 16.0f;

[self addChild:background];
[self addChild:_pirateShip];
[self addChild:_enemyShip];
[self addChild:buttonNext];
[self addChild:quad];
[self addChild:_message];
```

4. Update the `reset` method, as shown in the following code:

```
[_pirateShip moveToX:Sparrow.stage.width / 2
  andY:(Sparrow.stage.height / 2) - 20.0f withBlock:^{
  _message.text = @"There is your ship (the pirate ship) and at
    least one enemy";
  [_pirateShip.juggler delayInvocationByTime:2.5f block:^{
    [_pirateShip shootWithBlock:^{
      _message.text = @"Tap anywhere to move your ship.";
      [_pirateShip shootWithBlock:^{
        [_pirateShip shootWithBlock:^{
          _message.text = @"Double-tap on your ship to shoot.";
          [_pirateShip.juggler delayInvocationByTime:2.5f
            block:^{
            _message.text = @"In-between missions you can
              upgrade your ship.";
            [_pirateShip shoot];
          }];
        }];
      }];
    }];
  }];
}];
```

5. Run the example and when we see the intro, we now have hints displayed on the screen:

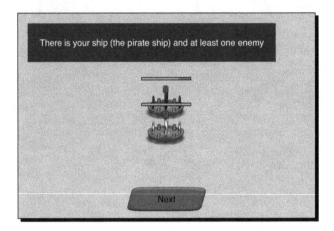

What just happened?

We first added an instance variable to display our hints. We then updated the initializer to initialize this instance variable and have a black but slightly opaque background. We added these two elements to the display tree.

In step 4, we updated the `reset` method to change the text of the message to show how the core gameplay elements work.

When we ran the example, the hints were displayed during the intro.

Loading and saving the current state

So far we can play the game, but as soon as we end the game, we have to start the game from the beginning.

Time for action – loading and saving the last played game

Follow these steps to load and save the current state:

1. In `World.h`, declare methods to serialize and deserialize data:
```
+(NSDictionary *) serialize;
+(void) deserialize: (NSDictionary *) dict;
```

2. Implement these serializers with the following lines of code:

```
+(NSDictionary *) serialize
{
    return @{
            @"level": [NSNumber numberWithInt:level],
            @"gold": [NSNumber numberWithInt:gold],
            @"damage": [NSNumber numberWithInt:damage],
            @"hitpoints": [NSNumber numberWithInt:hitpoints]
    };
}


+(void) deserialize: (NSDictionary *) dict
{
    level = [(NSNumber *) dict[@"level"] intValue];
    gold = [(NSNumber *) dict[@"gold"] intValue];
    damage = [(NSNumber *) dict[@"damage"] intValue];
    hitpoints = [(NSNumber *) dict[@"hitpoints"] intValue];
}
```

3. In `MainMenu.m`, add `World.h` to the import section and update the initializer:

```
buttonContinue.x = (Sparrow.stage.width - buttonContinue.width)
    / 2;
buttonContinue.y = 150.0f;
buttonContinue.enabled = NO;

NSUserDefaults *userDefaults = [NSUserDefaults
    standardUserDefaults];
id savedGame = [userDefaults objectForKey:@"game"];
if (savedGame != nil) {
    [World deserialize:(NSDictionary *) [userDefaults
        objectForKey:@"game"]];
    buttonContinue.enabled = YES;
}

[buttonContinue addEventListenerForType:SP_EVENT_TYPE_TRIGGERED
    block:^(id event) {
    [(SceneDirector *) self.director showScene:@"piratecove"];
}];

[self addChild:background];
```

4. In `AppDelegate.m`, we import `World.h` and add a new method, as shown in the following code:

```
- (void)applicationWillResignActiveNotification:(NSNotification*)
notification
{
    NSUserDefaults *userDefaults = [NSUserDefaults
standardUserDefaults];
    [userDefaults setObject:[World serialize] forKey:@"game"];
    [userDefaults synchronize];
}
```

5. Run the example to see the result. When we start the game, we can now continue the game:

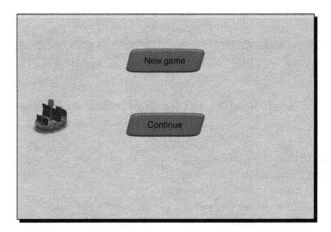

What just happened?

First, we added the serializer and deserializer methods to our `World` class. The serializer takes values from the `World` class and places them in `NSDictionary`. The deserializer works the other way around. It takes values from `NSDictionary` and updates the values in the `World` class.

In the main menu scene, we checked whether there is already something saved and we deserialize the data in case there is any data. We added an event listener for our **Continue** button, which directly switches to the pirate cove scene.

In step 4, we saved the game data once the application was not active any more.

When we ran the example, we were able to resume the game.

Pop quiz

Q1. When we override the font size for a bitmap font in SPTextField, it scales to that size.

1. True
2. False

Q2. When is it a good idea to encapsulate code snippets into their own class or methods?

1. Always, even if it's just used a single time
2. If the code snippet is being used multiple times
3. Never

Q3. `NSUserDefaults` provides a way to store data.

1. True
2. False

Summary

In this chapter, we learned about polishing our game. Specifically, we covered adding more scenes such as a main menu and an intro, and we touched upon tutorial mechanics.

Now that our game almost feels like an actual game, let's see how we can integrate third-party services—which is the topic of the next chapter.

11
Integrating Third-party Services

In the previous chapter, we polished our game by adding additional scenes and ironing out some of the quirks. After a game is over, it can now be restarted. Now that our game is pretty much finished, we need to apply some finishing touches, which will not influence the game directly, but its distribution and the experience the player has. If the user wants to play with their friends, we wouldn't need to implement a server and the networking mechanics by ourselves. There are services that take care of these problems; one of them is Apple Game Center.

In this chapter, we will integrate third-party services into our game. The following are the topics we will cover in this chapter:

- Getting the word out to potential testers
- The basic Game Center integration
- Showing different platforms for analytics

Getting word out to potential testers

Distributing to potential testers can be a daunting task. First, we would need to get the **Unique Device Identifier** (**UDID**) of each and every test device. We would then need to compile a special build that is restricted to only run on the devices whose UDID we provide in the provisioning profile used in the build. We would then need to send this special build to these testers, which they need to install using iTunes. After the beta testers have installed the application, we don't have any insight on how long they actually used the application and if the application crashes, they need to sync their device with iTunes and search for the crash report on the hard drive and send it to the developer. It's much better for the application to crash in the hand of beta testers than in the hands of actual customers.

For a long time, **TestFlight** has provided an easy solution for both collecting UDIDs and installing apps on your tester's devices. TestFlight provides an application for mobile devices that directly installs the application on the device instead of the user manually having to do so. TestFlight also has a web application that manages all of the devices, collects crash reports, and tracks the session.

The company behind TestFlight was acquired by Apple in February 2014, the result of which is that their SDK isn't allowed to be integrated into applications any more. The distribution component of TestFlight is still available for the time being.

Ubertesters is a very similar service that helps us to collect UDIDs of devices and helps testers to use our application. At the time of writing this book, Ubertesters is still in beta. While Ubertesters is a paid service, they do provide a free plan which only requires registering an account with them. The following is a screenshot of the Ubertesters website:

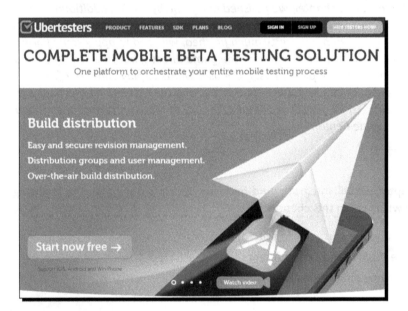

Registering at Ubertesters

In order to distribute our game with Ubertesters, we first need to register an account at `http://beta.ubertesters.com/sign_up`. Enter all the necessary data in the input fields.

We then need to create our own organization, where we can add our first application. Ubertesters guides us through this process when we register for the first time.

Let's call our application "Pirate Game" and choose iOS as its platform. Now, we are going to add our own devices; this is as simple as opening the URL `http://beta.ubertesters.com` in our mobile Safari browser following the instructions on the screen. This installs the Ubertesters app on our device and collects the UDID of the device.

After this, we see the device we just registered on the Ubertesters web interface where we get relevant data of the device such as the device name, its model, operating system, screen resolution, its locale, and the UDID.

It is also possible to set up over-the-air distribution, which means allowing testers to download the build from your site. Instructions for this setup can be found at this link: `http://aaronparecki.com/articles/2011/01/21/1/how-to-distribute-your-ios-apps-over-the-air`.

Integrating Ubertesters

Before we can get some beta testers, we need to integrate the Ubertesters SDK into our game. Only packages with the SDK integrated can be made available for testers.

Time for action – integrating Ubertesters

Use the following steps to integrate Ubertesters:

1. Open our Xcode project if it's not already open.
2. Download the Ubertesters SDK from `http://ubertesters.com/sdk/ubertesters.sdk.ios.zip`.
3. Extract the contents from the downloaded file somewhere on the hard drive.
4. Drag the extracted contents into the project file. They should be at the root level right at the same level as **Products**, **Frameworks**, and **Resources**.
5. Switch to the project configuration by clicking on the project's name in the project navigator. Inside the **General** tab, scroll down to **Linked Frameworks and Libraries**.
6. Add the following libraries by clicking on the plus button, selecting the correct library, and clicking on **Add**:
   - `AdSupport.framework`
   - `CoreImage.framework`
   - `SystemConfiguration.framework`
   - `CoreTelephony.framework`
   - `CoreLocation.framework`
   - `CoreMotion.framework`

7. Switch to the **Info** tab inside the project configuration.

8. Add a new key inside **Custom iOS Target Properties** by selecting any item and clicking on the plus button.

9. Call this key `ubertesters_project_id`.

10. As its value, use the ID from the Ubertesters website from the application from the **SDK Integration** tab.

11. Switch to `AppDelegate.m`.

12. Import the `Ubertesters` header file, using the following line of code:

```
#import <UbertestersSDK/Ubertesters.h>
```

13. Initialize the Ubertesters SDK by updating the `didFinishLaunchingWithOptions` method, as shown in the following code:

```
- (BOOL)application:(UIApplication *)application
  didFinishLaunchingWithOptions:(NSDictionary *)launchOptions
{
    CGRect screenBounds = [UIScreen mainScreen].bounds;
    _window = [[UIWindow alloc] initWithFrame:screenBounds];

    _viewController = [[SPViewController alloc] init];

    // Enable some common settings here:
    //
    // _viewController.showStats = YES;
    // _viewController.multitouchEnabled = YES;
    // _viewController.preferredFramesPerSecond = 60;

    [Ubertesters initialize];

    [_viewController startWithRoot:[Game class]
      supportHighResolutions:YES doubleOnPad:YES];

    [_window setRootViewController:_viewController];
    [_window makeKeyAndVisible];

    return YES;
}
```

14. Run the example.

When we start the example, we don't see any visible changes (refer to the following screenshot), which is an indicator that everything worked as we expected it to:

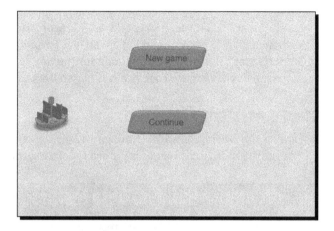

What just happened?

To get started, we opened our Xcode project, which is what we did in step 1.

Then, we downloaded the Ubertesters SDK and extracted the contents of the downloaded file. In step 4, we dragged the contents of the extracted file into the project itself. It should be on the root level directly below the project file itself on the same level as **Sparrow**, **Classes**, **Other Sources**, **Resources**, **Frameworks**, and **Products**.

In order to make the Ubertesters SDK work, we need to link against a variety of frameworks. In step 5, we switched to the general configuration by clicking on the **General** tab, where we can find the linked frameworks and libraries right at the bottom of the page. We added all the frameworks described in step 6.

Then, we added an entry to the PLIST file of the application itself. This can be done in the **Info** tab. We selected any entry under **Custom iOS Target Properties** and clicked on the plus button next to it. We then set the key name for this property, which we named `ubertesters_project_id`. We already have the project ID; we got it when we registered our application on Ubertesters. In the web interface of Ubertesters, this ID can be retrieved by clicking on **Projects**, then on our project (Pirate Game), and after this, on the **SDK Integration** tab on the left-hand side. These steps are necessary so that Ubertesters knows the application we registered in the web interface belongs to our game.

To use the SDK, we imported the Ubertesters SDK header file and initialized the SDK itself. This all happened inside the `AppDelegate` file in steps 11 to 13. We added the initialization of the SDK to where the application launches inside `didFinishLaunchingWithOptions`.

When we ran the example, there wasn't any visible change and the game ran as expected. When running the game on the actual device, it may take a bit longer to load, as the Ubertesters SDK checks against an Internet connection at startup. For production builds (for example, an App Store release), it is not recommended for the SDK to be included; the SDK should be included for the builds that are specifically going to beta testers.

Creating a build for beta testers

Now that we have integrated the Ubertesters SDK in our game, we can create a special build for our beta testers, which at the moment is just us, or more specifically, our own device.

Time for action – creating a build for beta testers

Us the following steps to create a special build for beta testers:

1. Log in to the provisioning portal at `https://developer.apple.com/account/ios/certificate/certificateList.action`.

2. In **Identifiers**, click on **App IDs**. Add a new one by clicking the plus button.

3. From **App ID Description**, choose **PirateGame**.

4. Set an **App ID Prefix** of your choice. All of the available prefixes will be shown as a drop-down list, where the default is **Team ID**. If you are unsure which one to use, use the default one.

5. In the **Bundle ID** input box, put in the bundle ID of our game. If you haven't chosen one, it's time to do so now. Make sure that the bundle ID is the same as **Bundle identifier** in the `App-Info.plist` file of our application. It is recommended that you use a reverse-domain name. Click on **Continue** and then **Done** to finish the process.

6. Show all devices by clicking on **All** in the **Devices** tab.

7. Add a new device by clicking on the plus button.

8. In **UDID**, enter the UDID of our device. This can be retrieved from the Ubertesters web application.

9. In **Provisioning Profiles**, select **Distribution** and add a new one by clicking the button with the plus icon.

10. Select **Ad Hoc** as the distribution type and click on **Continue**.

11. Select **App ID** we had created in step 5 and click on **Continue**.

12. If there isn't a certificate available, you will be asked to create a new certificate in the next step and select **App Store and Ad hoc**. Follow the instructions to generate the certificate. If there are already certificates available, you will be asked to choose one of them.

13. Open the newly created certificate and select the device we just added.

14. Generate the updated certificate.

15. In the Xcode project, select **iOS Device** as the target. This can be done through the build menu, where the product and the target are being displayed.

16. In the menu, select **Product** and click on **Archive**.

17. Open the Xcode organizer by clicking on **Window** and selecting **Organizer**.

18. Select the latest build and click on **Distribute**.

19. On the window that pops up, select **Save for Enterprise or Ad Hoc Deployment**. Confirm by clicking on **Next**.

20. Select the provisioning profile we created earlier.

21. Click on **Export** and save the package somewhere on the hard drive.

After we created the build, we return to the Xcode organizer, where we can either distribute the build again or validate it, as shown in the following screenshot:

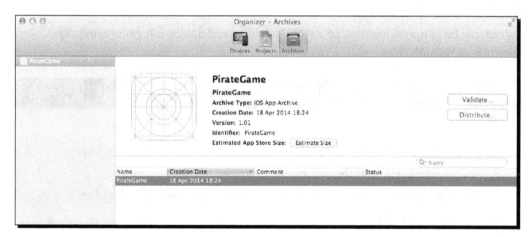

What just happened?

To create a special build for testers, we created an ad-hoc distribution profile just for our game. This is something we have to do just once per application, but not per build.

To create certificates, we needed the provisioning portal from the Apple developer member center. It consists of the following three tasks:

- **Creating an App ID**: This identifies our game (steps 2 to 5)
- **Adding a new device**: A distribution certificate can hold a number of target devices, which need to be added before the distribution certificate is created (steps 6 to 9)
- **Creating a distribution certificate**: This is used to sign the special build (steps 10 to 14)

Now that the certificate is generated, we created the build with the help of this certificate. We needed to select the **iOS Device** (or the name of the connected iOS device—if there is one). We selected a product to create an archive which we did in step 16. After the archive is created, we can select it from the Xcode organizer. We wanted to distribute this build, so that's why we clicked on the button with the **Distribute** label in step 18.

As we wanted an ad hoc deployment, we selected this option. **Ad hoc deployment** means that we are distributing our applications to a known number of devices, while a **distribution build**—such as for the Apple App Store—means the application can be installed on any number of devices that got the application from the Apple App Store. When we had the option to select a provisioning profile, we chose the one we created earlier. By clicking on **Export**, we got an IPA file that we had put in a safe place for the moment.

Deploying an application

Our special build is now finished, so we can go ahead and deploy our game using the Ubertesters web interface.

Time for action – deploying an application

To deploy the application, perform the following steps:

1. Log in to Ubertesters at `http://beta.ubertesters.com/sign_in`.
2. Click on **Projects** from the top menu.
3. Click on **Upload revision** and choose the special build we created earlier.
4. We can now enter a revision title and a description.
5. Select the revision we just uploaded.
6. Click on **Start** to allow this revision to be installed on the target devices.
7. On our registered device, we can now install our game.

   On the web interface, we can track the installations of our application, as shown in the following screenshot:

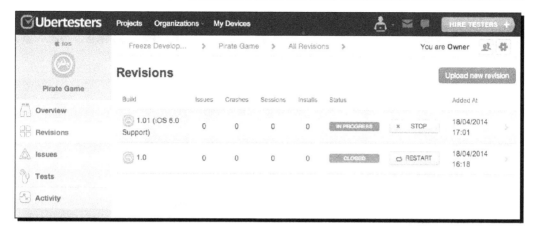

What just happened?

To deploy the application using Ubertesters, we logged in to Ubertesters first. When we see all the available projects, we can upload a new revision for each of the projects. At the moment, we only have one project.

After the revision is uploaded, we can optionally set a title and a description for the build. The following two things need to be considered when uploading a build:

◆ The Ubertesters SDK needs to be integrated in the application.

◆ The bundle version must be different for each uploaded revision. This setting can be found in the `Info.plist` file.

Before the application can be installed on the target devices, we need to start the process, which we did using the **Start** button. The testing phase can be stopped and restarted for every revision.

When we open the Ubertesters app in our registered device, we can now download our game. When our game is installed, we can run the game just as we expect it to.

Explaining Game Center

Game Center is a social media feature by Apple that allows leaderboards, achievements, and matchmaking. In a way, it's very similar to Steam for desktop platforms. Naturally, Game Center only works on iOS devices.

Integrating Game Center authentication

The first thing we need to do is authenticate Game Center to be able to use its features.

Time for action – integrating Game Center authentication

Use the following steps to integrate Game Center authentication:

1. Open our Xcode project if it's not already open.

2. Add `GameKit.framework` to the list of frameworks to be linked.

3. Switch to `AppDelegate.m`.

4. Import the `GameKit` header file using the following line of code:

   ```
   #import <GameKit/GameKit.h>
   ```

5. Update the `didFinishLaunchingWithOptions` method to look like the following piece of code:

   ```
   - (BOOL)application:(UIApplication *)application
     didFinishLaunchingWithOptions:(NSDictionary *)launchOptions
   {
       CGRect screenBounds = [UIScreen mainScreen].bounds;
       _window = [[UIWindow alloc] initWithFrame:screenBounds];

       _viewController = [[SPViewController alloc] init];

       [Ubertesters initialize];

       [_viewController startWithRoot:[Game class]
         supportHighResolutions:YES doubleOnPad:YES];

       [GKLocalPlayer localPlayer].authenticateHandler =
         ^(UIViewController *viewController, NSError *error) {
           if ([GKLocalPlayer localPlayer].authenticated) {
               NSLog(@"Already authenticated");
           } else if(viewController) {
               [[Sparrow currentController]
                 presentViewController:viewController animated:YES
                   completion:nil];//present the login form
           } else {
               NSLog(@"Problem while authenticating");
           }
       };

       [_window setRootViewController:_viewController];
       [_window makeKeyAndVisible];

       return YES;
   }
   ```

6. Run the example. If we are not authenticated yet, we should get a dialog to log in to **Game Center**:

What just happened?

To integrate Game Center, we linked the GameKit framework.

The next thing we did is update the `AppDelegate` class, and once more, it's the method that handles everything once the application has finished launching. In step 4, we needed to import the `GameKit` header.

In the next step, we authenticated Game Center right after we started the view controller with the `Game` class. The `localPlayer` returns the active player who interacts with the device.

We added an authentication handler that is called once Game Center is authenticated. If the player is already authenticated, we are just going to log in. The same happens if there is an error when the authentication fails.

If the player is not authenticated, we show the Game Center view controller through the current view controller from Sparrow.

Game Center is handled through iTunes Connect. The workflow is described at `https://developer.apple.com/library/ios/documentation/LanguagesUtilities/Conceptual/iTunesConnectGameCenter_Guide/Introduction/Introduction.html`.

If we want to use achievements in our game, we need to add all of our achievements in the iTunes Connect window shown in the following screenshot:

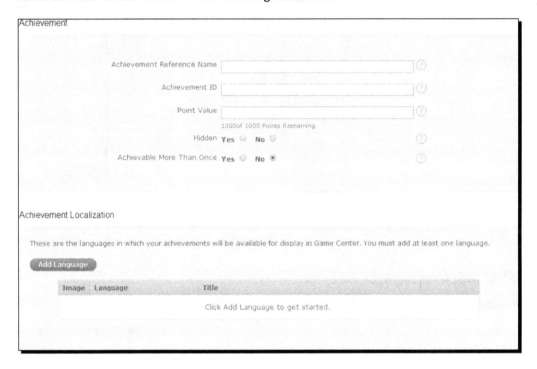

We would need a piece of code similar to the following code to set an achievement:

```
GKAchievement *achievement = [[GKAchievement alloc]
    initWithIdentifier: @"sankALotOfShips"];
if (achievement) {
    achievement.percentComplete = 100;
    [achievement reportAchievementWithCompletionHandler:^(NSError
        *error) {
        if (error != nil) {
            NSLog(@"Error in reporting achievements: %@", error);
        }
    }];
}
```

Let's assume we have an achievement called sankALotOfShips, which—as the name suggests—should be shown if our ship sank a whole lot of ships.

We retrieved the achievements and if the achievement exists, we set the achievement to be complete by simply adjusting the percentComplete property to 100. We then reported the updated achievement. If there was an error, we logged it to the console.

To learn more about achievements in Game Center, take a look at `https://developer.apple.com/library/ios/documentation/NetworkingInternet/Conceptual/GameKit_Guide/Achievements/Achievements.html`.

Have a go hero

Game Center has quite a big arsenal of things to do. The following are some suggestions of what could be done:

◆ Currently, we only log if the player is already authenticated or the authentication failed because the player canceled the authentication. This can be improved with some basic error handling.

◆ Game Center also provides leaderboards. As our game is very much highscore-based or gold-based to be more accurate, you could try to utilize this functionality to add leaderboards to our game. If you are not too afraid about performing some refactoring, you might even want to introduce a highscore-based system that doesn't rely on gold. This is definitely a harder, but a more balanced way to go, as the player shouldn't be punished for using in-game currency to upgrade their gear. Take a look at the official Apple documentation at `https://developer.apple.com/library/ios/documentation/NetworkingInternet/Conceptual/GameKit_Guide/LeaderBoards/LeaderBoards.html` to learn more about leaderboards.

◆ Since the preceding task is definitely much more difficult and a bit far fetched, you can try to use matchmaking abilities to let two players battle against each other. This will lead to a major refactoring of the existing code though. A good starting point will be to take a look at the matchmaking documentation at `https://developer.apple.com/library/ios/documentation/NetworkingInternet/Conceptual/GameKit_Guide/MatchmakingwithGameCenter/MatchmakingwithGameCenter.html`.

An overview of analytics services

Some basic analytics are most likely provided by a beta distribution service (as Ubertesters in our case). When you have a paid app in the Apple App Store, it is often necessary to have detailed information, such as how many in-app purchases there were and accurate details about play sessions.

Analytics are usually a paid service; in most cases, there is either a free or a trial version. Let's take a look at two analytics services.

Flurry analytics

Flurry is a service that has been around for a few years and provides support for multiple platforms. It provides the following features:

- Geographical data of users
- Crash analytics
- Play session statistics

Flox

Flox is a service made by Gamua, the guys behind the Sparrow framework. Flox is a relatively new service which is available at `http://gamua.com/flox/`.

Flox provides the following features:

- Remote logging
- Leaderboards
- Save games
- Session and user statistics

The Objective-C headers are available at `https://github.com/Gamua/Flox-ObjC`. It even offers Game Center integration.

Let's take a look at what Flox integration would look like. The next step after registering on the Flox service is to create a game. We get its game ID and its game key.

After integrating the Flox SDK into our game, we will need to initialize Flox inside our application delegate (`AppDelegate.m`), using the following code:

```
[Flox startWithGameID:@"gameID" key:@"gameKey" version:@"1.0"];
```

After this, we can dispatch events that will show up in the Flox web interface:

```
[Flox logEvent:@"GameStarted"];
```

If we wanted to use leaderboards through Flox, we will need to create the leaderboard itself using the web interface. If we want to load all scores from the leaderboards, the following piece of code will set us up:

```
[Flox loadScoresFromLeaderboard:@"default"
  timeScope:FXTimeScopeAllTime onComplete:^(NSArray *scores, NSError
    *error)
{
    NSLog(@"So much scores. Got %d", (int)scores.count);
}];
```

To save to the leaderboards, we can use the following piece of code:

```
[Flox postScore:World.gold ofPlayer:@"playerName"
  toLeaderboard:@"default"];
```

Pop quiz

Q1. What is Ubertesters?

1. It allows private applications for beta testers to be distributed
2. It is a platform to search for beta testers
3. It is an online magazine that tests mobile applications

Q2. What is Game Center?

1. Apple's solution for a game's social features such as achievements and high score lists
2. A publisher for mobile games
3. Games that work on multiple platforms

Q3. What does an analytics platform usually provide?

1. Private data of users
2. Anonymous play sessions
3. Statistical data

Summary

In this chapter, we learned about integrating third-party services into our game, especially to distribute our game and integrate it with Apple's Game Center.

Our game is now finished. Of course, there are a lot of things that we could still add or update, but all in all, we mastered the process of creating a playable game during the course of this book while learning about the Sparrow framework as well as distributing our application and creating game assets.

Pop Quiz Answers

Chapter 1, Getting Started with Sparrow

Pop quiz	
Q1	1
Q2	3
Q3	1

Chapter 2, Displaying Our First Objects

Pop quiz	
Q1	3
Q2	2
Q3	2

Chapter 3, Managing Assets and Scenes

Pop quiz	
Q1	1
Q2	2
Q3	2

Chapter 4, The Basics of Our Game

Pop quiz	
Q1	2
Q2	1 and 3
Q3	1
Q4	3

Chapter 5, Beautifying Our Game

Pop quiz	
Q1	1
Q2	2
Q3	1

Chapter 6, Adding Game Logic

Pop quiz	
Q1	3
Q2	2
Q3	2

Chapter 7, User Interface

Pop quiz	
Q1	1
Q2	1
Q3	3

Chapter 8, Artificial Intelligence and Game Progression

Pop quiz	
Q1	1
Q2	2
Q3	2

Chapter 9, Adding Audio to Our Game

Pop quiz	
Q1	1
Q2	2
Q3	1

Chapter 10, Polishing Our Game

Pop quiz	
Q1	1
Q2	2
Q3	1

Chapter 11, Integrating Third-party Services

Pop quiz	
Q1	1
Q2	1
Q3	2

Afterword

If you intend to publish a game on the Apple App Store, you should invest an extra amount of polish to get all the details right. This includes creating an icon and splash screens for all devices, getting the bundle identifiers, bundle version, and bundle names right. If your game allows switching its orientation from landscape to portrait or vice versa, you should make sure that it does so without any side effects. You should also double-check if all the graphics are being displayed correctly on all the target devices.

Index

Ubertesters SDK
  URL 231
Unique Device Identifier (UDID) 229
utility functions 34
util, sparrow folder 12

V

viewport
  scaling 71, 72

W

win condition
  adding 193-195
World class
  implementing 184, 185

X

Xcode
  downloading 9, 10
  Sparrow API documentation, adding to 21
  URL 21

Thank you for buying
Sparrow iOS Game Framework Beginner's Guide

About Packt Publishing

Packt, pronounced 'packed', published its first book "*Mastering phpMyAdmin for Effective MySQL Management*" in April 2004 and subsequently continued to specialize in publishing highly focused books on specific technologies and solutions.

Our books and publications share the experiences of your fellow IT professionals in adapting and customizing today's systems, applications, and frameworks. Our solution based books give you the knowledge and power to customize the software and technologies you're using to get the job done. Packt books are more specific and less general than the IT books you have seen in the past. Our unique business model allows us to bring you more focused information, giving you more of what you need to know, and less of what you don't.

Packt is a modern, yet unique publishing company, which focuses on producing quality, cutting-edge books for communities of developers, administrators, and newbies alike. For more information, please visit our website: www.packtpub.com.

About Packt Open Source

In 2010, Packt launched two new brands, Packt Open Source and Packt Enterprise, in order to continue its focus on specialization. This book is part of the Packt Open Source brand, home to books published on software built around Open Source licences, and offering information to anybody from advanced developers to budding web designers. The Open Source brand also runs Packt's Open Source Royalty Scheme, by which Packt gives a royalty to each Open Source project about whose software a book is sold.

Writing for Packt

We welcome all inquiries from people who are interested in authoring. Book proposals should be sent to author@packtpub.com. If your book idea is still at an early stage and you would like to discuss it first before writing a formal book proposal, contact us; one of our commissioning editors will get in touch with you.

We're not just looking for published authors; if you have strong technical skills but no writing experience, our experienced editors can help you develop a writing career, or simply get some additional reward for your expertise.

Sencha Touch Cookbook

ISBN: 978-1-84951-544-3   Paperback: 350 pages

Over 100 recipes for creating HTML5-based cross-platform apps for touch devices

1. Master cross-platform application development.

2. Incorporate geo location into your apps.

3. Develop native looking web apps.

PhoneGap Beginner's Guide

ISBN: 978-1-84951-536-8   Paperback: 328 pages

Build cross-platform mobile applications with the PhoneGap open source development framework

1. Learn how to use the PhoneGap mobile application framework.

2. Develop cross-platform code for iOS, Android, BlackBerry, and more.

3. Write robust and extensible JavaScript code.

4. Master new HTML5 and CSS3 APIs.

Please check **www.PacktPub.com** for information on our titles

Rhomobile Beginner's Guide

ISBN: 978-1-84951-516-0   Paperback: 264 pages

Step-by-step instructions to build an enterprise mobile web application from scratch

1. Explore all of Rhomobile's features and products through the creation of a mobile web application.

2. Step-by-step instructions help you to build an enterprise mobile web application from scratch, through deployment.

3. Clear guides for developing applications on iPhone, Blackberry, and other smartphones.

Creating Games with cocos2d for iPhone 2

ISBN: 978-1-84951-900-7   Paperback: 388 pages

Master cocos2d through building nine complete games for the iPhone

1. Games are explained in detail, from the design decisions to the code itself.

2. Learn to build a wide variety of game types, from a memory tile game to an endless runner.

3. Use different design approaches to help you explore the cocos2d framework.

Please check **www.PacktPub.com** for information on our titles

www.ingramcontent.com/pod-product-compliance
Lightning Source LLC
Chambersburg PA
CBHW060530060326
40690CB00017B/3446